Pocket Change Treasure Hunt:

Doubled Die Quarters

Author's Note:

First and foremost, I would like to give all the thanks and glory of completion of my book to God Almighty. He has greatly blessed me with discovering and identifying the doubled die quarters featured in this book, and has given me the confidence and determination needed to see my goal through to the end. I also want to let my family know how much I love and appreciate them for their support of me, and for their enthusiasm in my interest of coins.

The Excitement of a Treasure Hunt Without the Hassle

The thrill of uncovering treasures, the joy of discovering something new, and the reward of finding what you are searching for; without the cost! This is what you can experience when checking your pocket change for doubled die quarters. Discover how the quarters we spend everyday are comprised of a multitude of unique doubled die coins. Clearly see how a doubled die quarter is a standout treasure compared to a normal quarter. If a doubled die quarter is found celebrate ☺; if the quarter is normal, realize it costs you nothing and can be spent as 25¢ USD. No need for a large exploration team, no need to traverse harsh seas and landscapes, and no need to invest in highly expensive equipment; just look at your quarters from the comfort of your home!

HAPPY TREASURE HUNTING!!!

Doubled Die Identification, Illustrations, and Terminology Used in this Book:

Understanding the KENC™ Catalogue Identification System:

KENC 25¢ 2005 P MN DDO-001/DDR-001

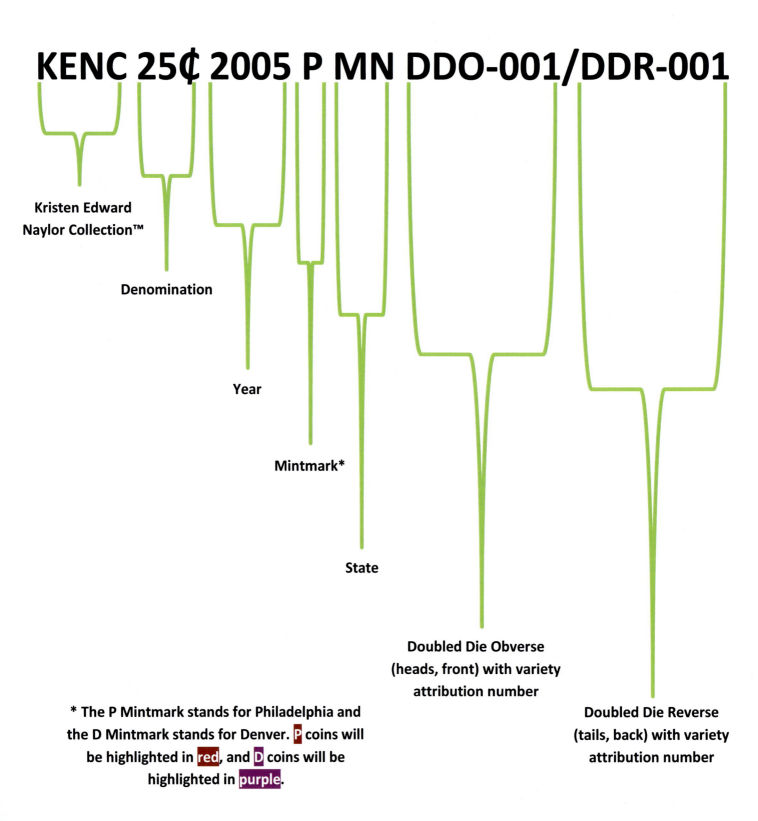

Kristen Edward Naylor Collection™

Denomination

Year

Mintmark*

State

Doubled Die Obverse (heads, front) with variety attribution number

Doubled Die Reverse (tails, back) with variety attribution number

* The P Mintmark stands for Philadelphia and the D Mintmark stands for Denver. P coins will be highlighted in red, and D coins will be highlighted in purple.

Locating the Mintmark

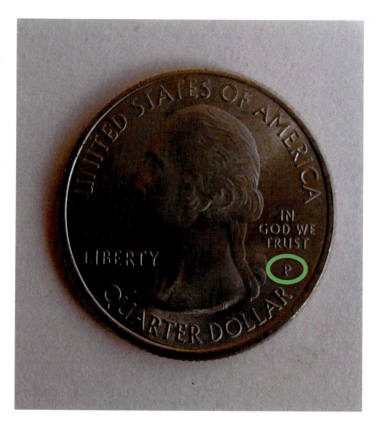 

The mintmark can be found on the obverse (heads, front) of the coin.
It appears near the bottom right underneath IN GOD WE TRUST.
P stands for Philadelphia, and D stands for Denver.

*When looking for a particular KENC™ doubled die, be sure that
the coin has the same mintmark as listed in the catalogue entry. If
the doubling and mintmark for a specific coin match, it is the
KENC™ doubled die listed. If the doubling for a specific coin
matches the KENC™ catalogue entry but the mintmarks do not
match; the coin would be a new or different doubled die.

Symbols Used in This Book

Blue arrows point out the doubling on a coin.

Yellow arrows point out die indicators for a particular doubled die, if die indicators are present on the coin*

Green arrows point out something specific about the doubled die coin to differentiate it from similar doubled die coin(s).

*The same doubled die coin may or may not have the die indicators pointed out depending upon how early or late the doubled die was in its use life during the striking process. Die indicators that are not pointed out may be present on the same doubled die coin if it is a later die state.

Rotate the coin a quarter turn to the right (clockwise) to see the doubling clearer.

Rotate the coin a quarter turn to the left (counterclockwise) to see the doubling clearer.

Turn the coin upside down (invert) to see the doubling clearer.

Gradually turn the coin to see different areas of doubling at clearer angles. (This is helpful on coins with doubling scattered over much of the design).

Helping Us Keep an Eye Out for Doubled Dies:

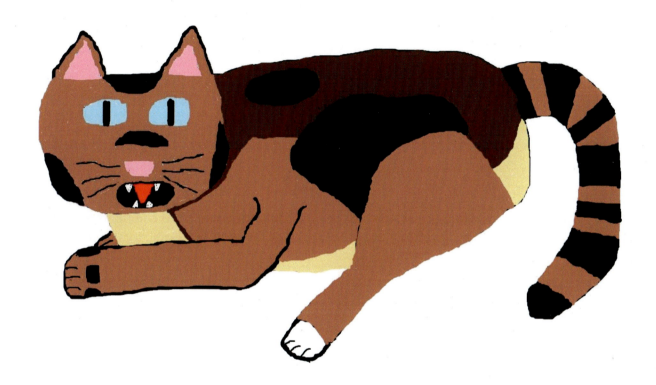

Numis the Numismatist Cat™

Numis™ Eye Appeal Scale

 **Detectable**- With careful examination of the coin, the doubling can be seen.

 **Noticeable**- A small amount of doubling that can be seen with magnification.

 **Standard**- A good amount of doubling that can be clearly seen. This can be with or without magnification being required.

 **Premium**- A large amount of doubling over multiple areas or strong doubling that is clearly seen. This can be with or without magnification being required.

 **Amazing**- An extreme amount of doubling over multiple areas or very strong doubling that stands out prominently. This can be with or without magnification being required.

Key Terms

Die- The device which strikes the image of the coin into the planchet. The image on the die is opposite of how it will appear on the finished coin. Sunk-in or incuse areas on the die will appear raised on the coin and raised areas on the die will appear sunk-in or incuse on the coin.

Planchet- The metal disk which the die strikes the coin image into and what ultimately becomes the finished coin

Doubled Die- A coin which exhibits extra design element(s) as a result of the die that struck it containing and transferring the image with those extra design element(s)

Die Chip- A small area of the die becomes removed from stress, wear, and/or damage. When the die strikes the planchet metal flows into the removed area producing a raised "mound" (Die chips often have a craggy, blobby look about them and almost look as if they fell and splattered onto the coin).

Die Break- A large area of the die becomes removed from stress, wear, and/or damage. When the die strikes the planchet metal flows into the removed area producing a raised "mound" (Die breaks often have a craggy, blobby look about them and almost look as if they fell and splattered onto the coin).

Die Crack- A thin break in the die which will produce a raised line as metal flows into it when the die strikes the planchet

Strike Doubling- The design elements of the coin look similar to that of a doubled die, but this appearance is a result of movement during the striking process, rather than actual extra design elements being present on the die striking the planchet. A shift/pull or momentum towards a particular direction during the strike can give the appearance of a flat "sheet of ice" that the design "slid" on. A strong abrupt movement or force of impact during the strike can give the design a cut-into or step-down appearance. (These coins are NOT considered doubled dies. However, if the coin appeals to you, put it in your collection).

Illustrations of Terms on Following Pages:

Here is a normal die (lid) with a
rectangle as its design.

The die is striking the planchet (clay disk) straight
down without any shifting or movement.

The resulting die strike will produce a normal coin
with the design appearing as intended.

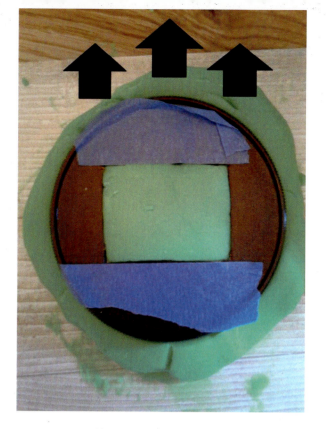 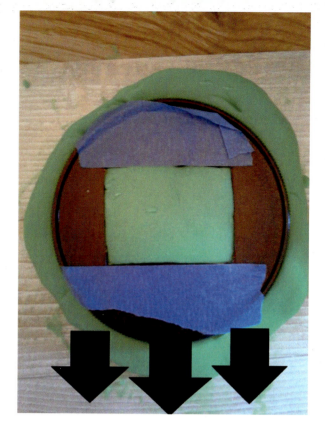

Here again is a normal die striking a planchet. However, while striking there is a shift/pull or momentum toward a particular direction.

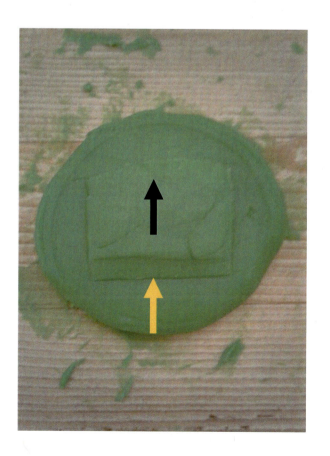 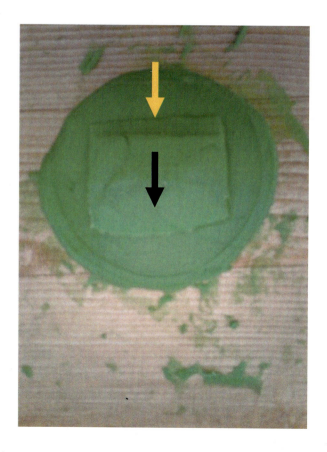

The resulting die strike will produce a coin with strike doubling appearing on it. The strike doubling (pointed out with the orange arrows) will look like a flat "sheet of ice" that the design "slid" on.

Here is a normal 1999 P Pennsylvania quarter with the letters and design appearing as intended.

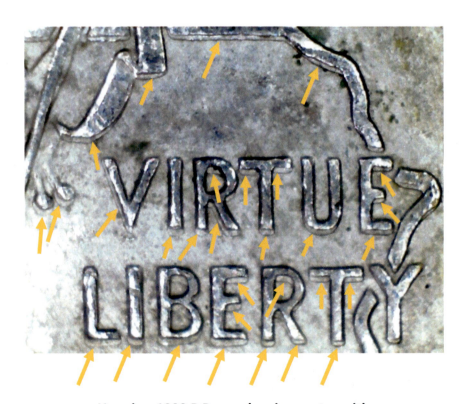

Here is a 1999 P Pennsylvania quarter with strike doubling. The letters and design of the coin appear to have "slid" on a flat "sheet of ice." Orange arrows point out the strike doubling.

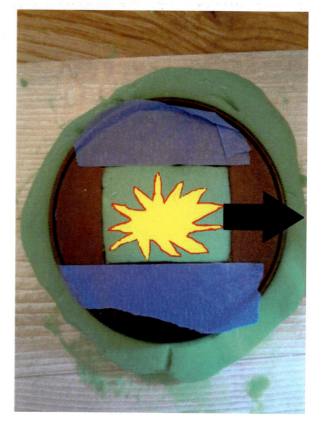

The same normal die is striking a planchet. During the strike there is a strong abrupt movement or force of impact.

The resulting die strike will produce a coin with strike doubling appearing on it. The strike doubling (pointed out with orange arrows) will look like a cut-in or step-down on the design.

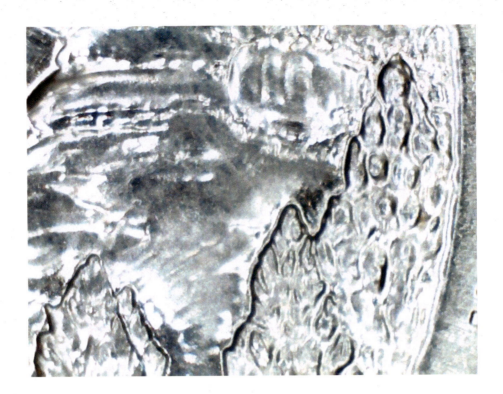

Here is a normal 2016 P Illinois
Shawnee quarter with the tree design
appearing as intended.

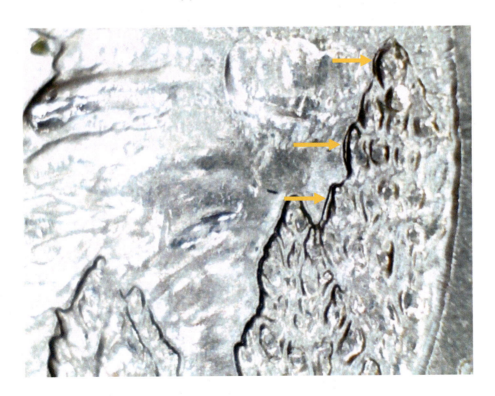

Here is a 2016 P Illinois Shawnee quarter
with strike doubling. The tree design of the
coin appears as though it was cut into. Note
how the strike doubling appears "lower"
like a step-down from the design. Orange
arrows point out the strike doubling.

Here is a doubled die. There is an extra second
bottom of the rectangle design present on the die
(pointed out with a blue arrow).

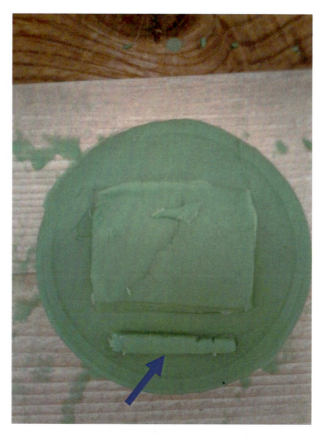

The resulting die strike will produce a doubled die coin
with the extra bottom of the rectangle showing up on
the coin (pointed out with a blue arrow).

Here is the doubled die with a small area of the die having been removed from stress and wear (pointed out with a yellow arrow).

Here is the doubled die with a large area of the die having been removed from even further stress and wear (pointed out with a yellow arrow).

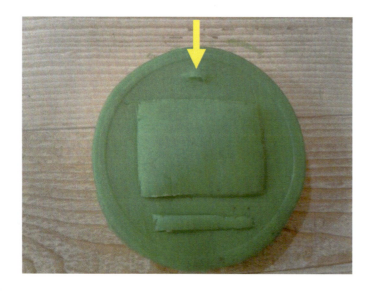

The resulting die strike will produce a doubled die coin with a die chip appearing on it (pointed out with a yellow arrow).

The resulting die strike will produce a doubled die coin with a die break appearing on it (pointed out with a yellow arrow).

Here is the doubled die with a die break, which now also has a thin break near the upper corner of the rectangle design (pointed out with yellow arrows.)

The resulting die strike will produce a doubled die coin with a die break, and now a thin raised line known as a die crack (pointed out with yellow arrows) will also show up on the coin.

Revealing Doubled Dies:

Lighting and Magnification:

When looking for doubled dies, having the proper lighting and magnification will go a long way. A nice even light over the coin will allow doubling to be seen, while lighting that is too dull or bright will conceal the doubling in shadows and glare. The use of a coin loupe or magnifying glass will enlarge the image of the coin enough to see most doubled dies. Having a clearer, more detailed look at the coin will reveal doubled dies not easily seen by the naked eye, and possibly uncover even more doubling on doubled dies that can be seen with the eye.

Dim/Dull Lighting Without Magnification:

Here is **KENC 25¢ 2015 P NE DDR-034.** The coin appears dull and muted, and no doubling stands out.

Bright Light at an Angle Without Magnification:

Here is the same **KENC 25¢ 2015 P NE DDR-034.**
The coin appears very bright and produces a glare.
No doubling stands out.

Natural/Normal Even Lighting Without Magnification:

Again, here is the same **KENC 25¢ 2015 P NE DDR-034.**
The coin looks natural, and the image is clear. Doubling
can be detected above the water pump and along the
right side of window 6.

Natural/Normal Even Lightning With Magnification:

Once more, here is the same **KENC 25¢ 2015 P NE DDR-034.**
The coin looks natural, and the image is clear. Doubling can
be clearly seen above the water pump and along the right
side and bottom of window 6.

Sneak Peek:

KENC 25¢ 2015 P NE DDR-034 is an amazing doubled die which can be seen with the naked eye and has prominent doubling both in the window and above the water pump. This was a clear choice to use when illustrating the importance of proper lighting and how magnification can help show the full extent of doubling present. This and many other doubled dies will be featured in future publications.

KENC 25¢ 2015 P NE DDR-034

Description: Strong doubling shows above the water pump. Strong doubling shows along the right side and bottom of window 6.

Die Indicators: Obverse none observed

Reverse none observed

Have an Example for Comparison:

When looking for doubled dies keeping a quality example of each normal coin design can be a great help. A suspected doubled die coin can be compared to the normal coin example to see if the suspected doubling is truly a doubled die, or just part of the intended design. The normal coin example does not need to be in perfect condition, but it should clearly show all the details of the coin design, and be free of heavy contact marks, scratches, and/or damage that remove or alter key areas of the coin design.

DOUBLED DIES

1999 Delaware

Area(s) of Interest:

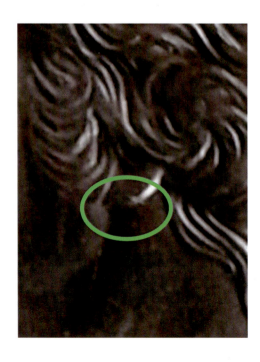

Below Washington's ear

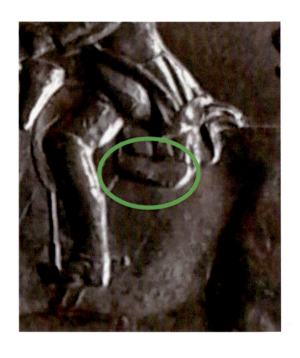

Below the saddlebag

KENC 25¢ 1999 P DE DDO-001

Description: Doubling shows below Washington's ear.

Die Indicators: Obverse A die crack starts left of and goes through the base of Washington's neck.

Reverse none observed

KENC 25¢ 1999 P DE DDO-002

Description: Doubling shows below Washington's ear.

Die Indicators: Obverse none observed

Reverse none observed

KENC 25¢ 1999 P DE DDR-001

Description: Doubling shows below the saddlebag.

Die Indicators: Obverse none observed

Reverse none observed

KENC 25¢ 1999 D DE DDO-001

Description: Strong doubling shows below Washington's ear.

Die Indicators: Obverse none observed

Reverse none observed

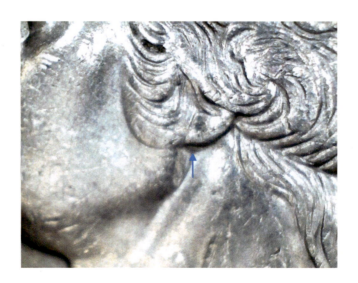

1999 Pennsylvania

Area(s) of Interest:

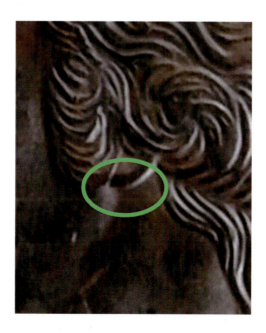

Below Washington's ear

Description: Doubling shows below Washington's ear.

Die Indicators: Obverse A die chip appears in the upper opening of the B in LIBERTY.

Reverse none observed

Description: Doubling shows below Washington's ear.

Die Indicators: Obverse none observed

Reverse none observed

1999 Georgia

Area(s) of Interest:

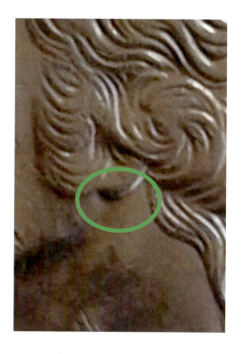

Below Washington's ear

Description: Strong doubling appears below Washington's ear.

Die Indicators: Obverse none observed

Reverse none observed

2000 Maryland

Area(s) of Interest:

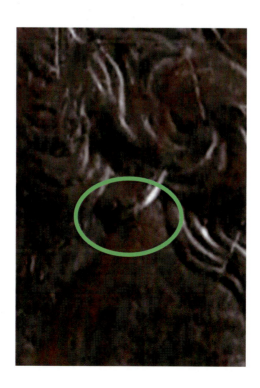

Below Washington's ear

Description: Doubling shows below Washington's ear.

Die Indicators: Obverse none observed

Reverse none observed

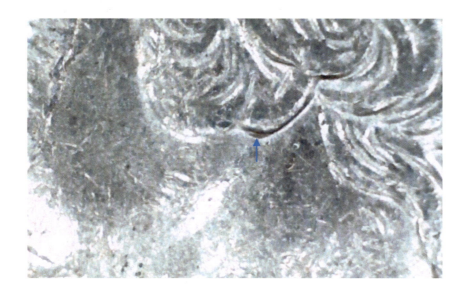

2000 New Hampshire

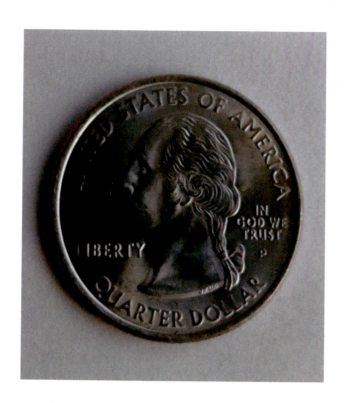 

Area(s) of Interest:

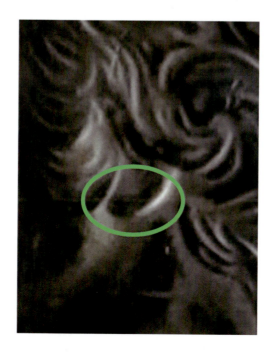

Below Washington's ear

Description: Very strong doubling shows below Washington's ear.

Die Indicators: Obverse none observed

Reverse none observed

2000 Virginia

Area(s) of Interest:

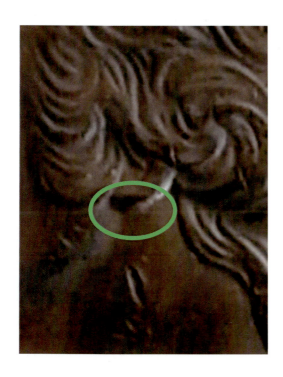

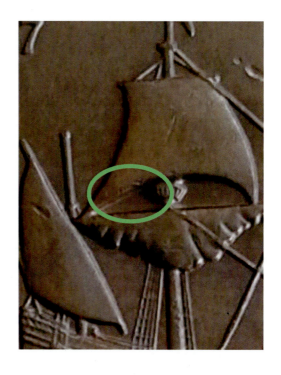

Below Washington's ear

Beneath the sail of the ship

KENC 25¢ 2000 P VA DDO-001

Description: Doubling shows below Washington's ear.

Die Indicators: Obverse none observed

                       Reverse none observed

KENC 25¢ 2000 P VA DDR-001

Description: Doubling shows beneath the sail of the ship in the foreground.

Die Indicators: Obverse A die crack starts left of and goes through the top of the designer's initials JF.

                       Reverse none observed

2001 North Carolina

Area(s) of Interest:

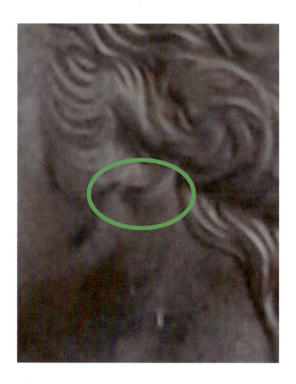

Below Washington's ear

Description: Strong doubling shows below Washington's ear.

Die Indicators: Obverse none observed

Reverse none observed

Description: Doubling shows below Washington's ear.

Die Indicators: Obverse none observed

Reverse none observed

2001 Rhode Island

Area(s) of Interest:

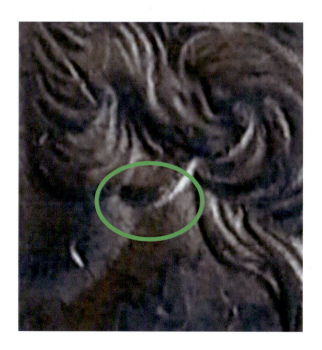

Below Washington's ear

Description: Doubling shows below Washington's ear.

Die Indicators: Obverse none observed

Reverse none observed

Description: Doubling shows below Washington's ear.

Die Indicators: Obverse none observed

Reverse none observed

2001 Vermont

Area(s) of Interest:

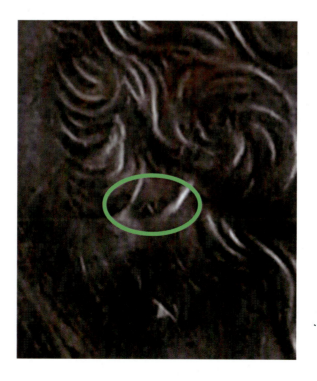

Below Washington's ear

Description: Doubling shows below Washington's ear.

Die Indicators: Obverse none observed

Reverse none observed

2001 Kentucky

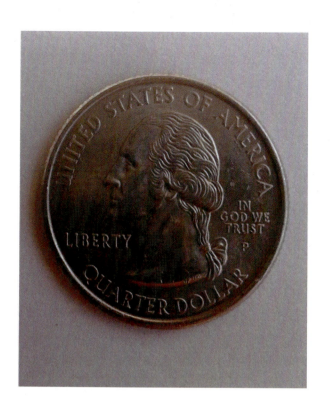 

Area(s) of Interest:

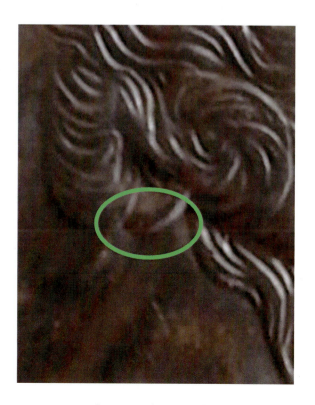

Below Washington's ear

Description: Strong doubling shows below Washington's ear.

Die Indicators: Obverse none observed

Reverse none observed

2002 Tennessee

Area(s) of Interest:

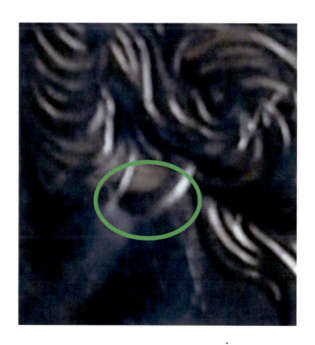

Below Washington's ear

KENC 25¢ 2002 P TN DDO-001

Description: Doubling shows below Washington's ear.

Die Indicators: Obverse none observed

Reverse none observed

KENC 25¢ 2002 D TN DDO-001

Description: Very strong doubling shows below Washington's ear.

Die Indicators: Obverse none observed

Reverse none observed

2002 Ohio

Area(s) of Interest:

Below Washington's ear

Description: Very strong doubling shows below Washington's ear.

Die Indicators: Obverse none observed

                Reverse none observed

2002 Louisiana

Area(s) of Interest:

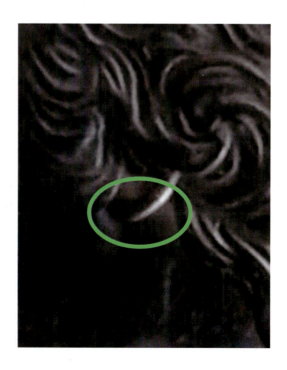

Below Washington's ear

Description: Very strong doubling shows below Washington's ear.

Die Indicators: **Obverse** none observed

Reverse none observed

2002 Indiana

Area(s) of Interest:

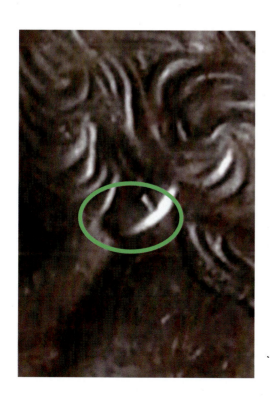 

Below Washington's ear   Underneath the front of the racecar

Description: Close doubling shows below Washington's ear.

Die Indicators: Obverse none observed

Reverse none observed

Description: Doubling shows underneath the front of the racecar.

Die Indicators: Obverse none observed

Reverse none observed

Description: Doubling shows underneath the front of the racecar near the left edge of the state outline.

Die Indicators: Obverse none observed

Reverse none observed

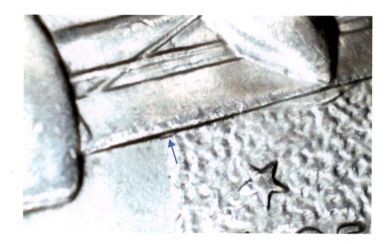

2002 Mississippi

Area(s) of Interest:

**Along the left side of the large leaf appearing below
the M in Magnolia**

Description: Doubling shows along the left side of the large leaf that appears below the M in Magnolia.

Die Indicators: Obverse none observed

Reverse none observed

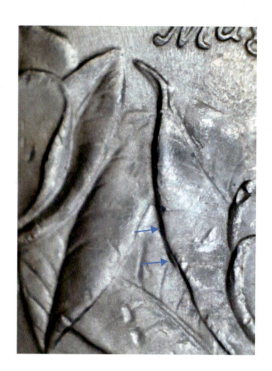

2003 Maine

Area(s) of Interest:

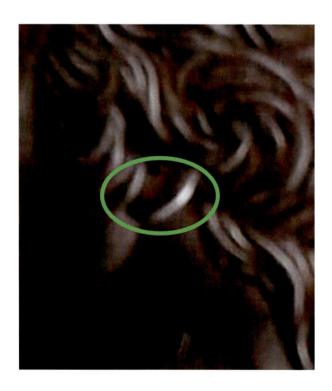 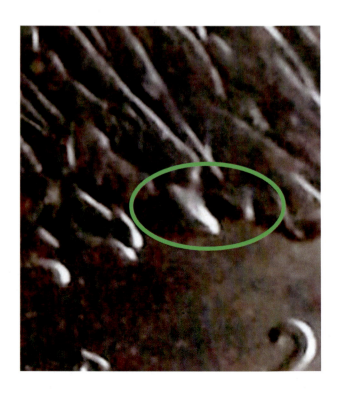

Below Washington's ear   The rocks at the water's edge

Description: Doubling shows below Washington's ear.

Die Indicators: Obverse none observed

Reverse none observed

KENC 25¢ 2003 D ME DDR-001

Description: Strong doubling shows below the rocks at the water's edge.

Die Indicators: Obverse none observed

Reverse none observed

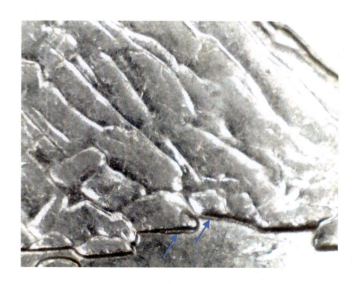

KENC 25¢ 2003 D ME DDR-002

Description: Doubling shows below the rock at the water's edge.

Die Indicators: Obverse none observed

Reverse none observed

KENC 25¢ 2003 D ME DDR-003

Description: Close doubling shows below the rock at the water's edge.

Die Indicators: Obverse A die crack starts left of and goes through the base of Washington's neck.

Reverse none observed

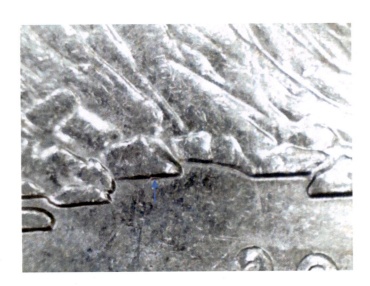 

2004 Michigan

Area(s) of Interest:

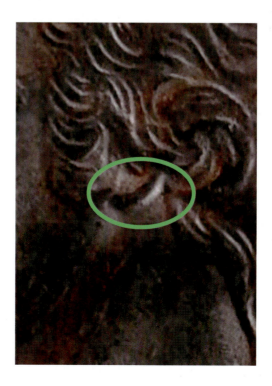

Below Washington's ear

Description: Strong doubling shows below Washington's ear.

Die Indicators: Obverse none observed

Reverse none observed

2004 Florida

Area(s) of Interest:

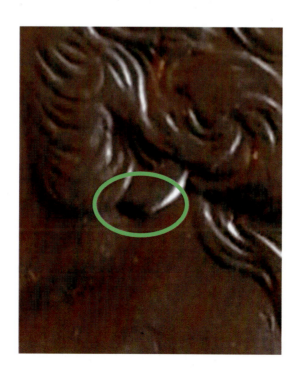

Below Washington's ear

Description: Doubling shows below Washington's ear.

Die Indicators: Obverse none observed

Reverse none observed

2004 Texas

Area(s) of Interest:

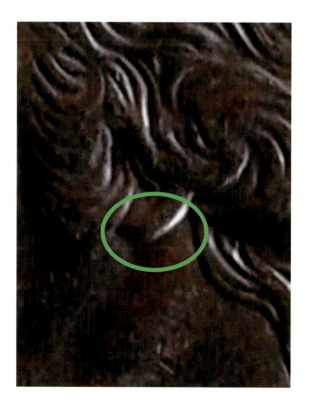

Below Washington's ear

Description: Doubling shows below Washington's ear.

Die Indicators: Obverse none observed

Reverse none observed

2004 Iowa

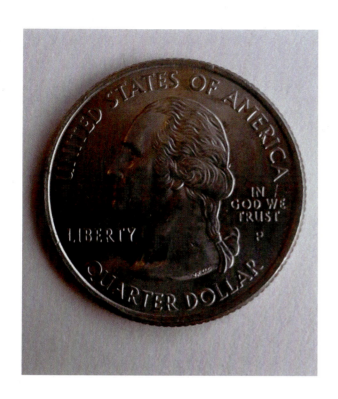

Area(s) of Interest:

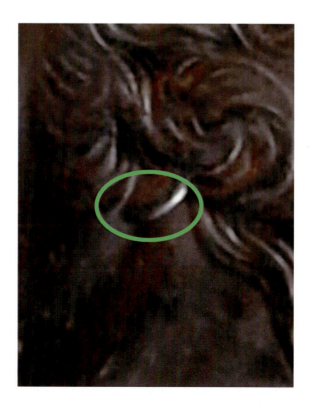

Below Washington's ear

Description: Doubling shows below Washington's ear.

Die Indicators: Obverse none observed

Reverse none observed

Description: Doubling shows below Washington's ear.

Die Indicators: Obverse none observed

Reverse none observed

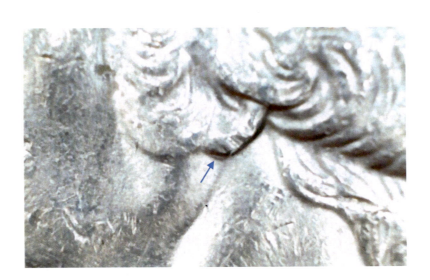

2004 Wisconsin

Area(s) of Interest:

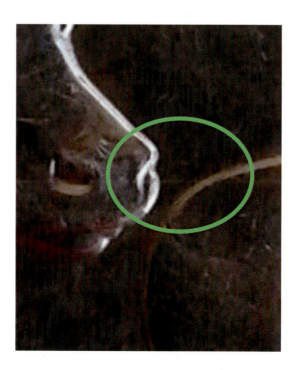

The cow's nostril, The edge of the cheese wheel

Description: Doubling shows along the right side of the cow's nose.

Die Indicators: Obverse A die chip appears on the designer's initials JF.

Reverse none observed

Description: Doubling shows in the cow's nostril.

Die Indicators: Obverse none observed

Reverse none observed

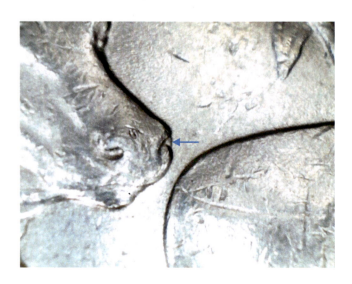

Description: Minor doubling shows on the cheese wheel, just right of the cow's nose.

Die Indicators: Obverse none observed

Reverse none observed

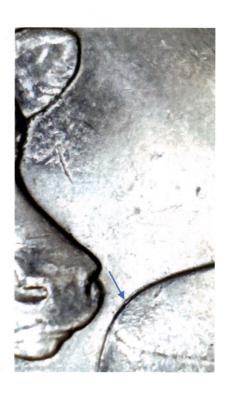

KENC 25¢ 2004 D WI DDR-001

Description: Doubling shows along the inside of the cow's nostril.

Die Indicators: Obverse none observed

Reverse none observed

2005 California

Area(s) of Interest:

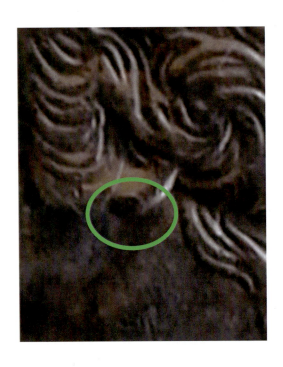

Below Washington's ear

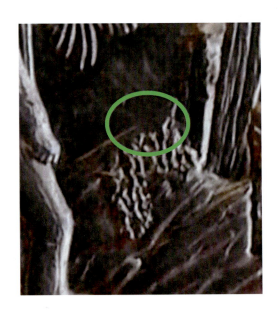

Above the trees in the distance

Description: Doubling shows below Washington's ear.

Die Indicators: Obverse none observed

Reverse none observed

Description: Strong doubling shows below Washington's ear.

Die Indicators: Obverse none observed

Reverse none observed

Description: Doubling shows as an extra tree in the distance.

Die Indicators: Obverse none observed

Reverse none observed

2005 Minnesota

Area(s) of Interest:

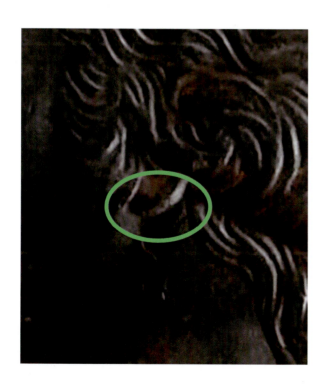 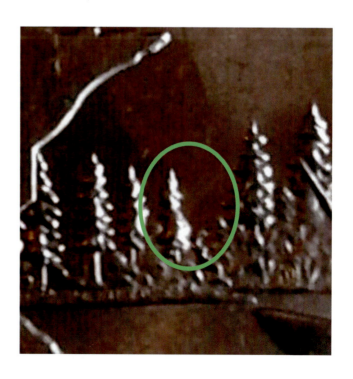

Below Washington's ear

Near the tree whose top lines up with the top right point of the state outline

KENC 25¢ 2005 P MN DDO-001/DDR-001

Description: Doubling shows below Washington's ear. Doubling shows along the bottom right of the tree whose top lines up with the top right point of the state outline.

Die Indicators: Obverse A die chip shows between the designers' initials JF, WC.

Reverse none observed

KENC 25¢ 2005 P MN DDO-002

Description: Close doubling shows below Washington's ear.

Die Indicators: Obverse none observed

Reverse none observed

Description: Doubling shows below Washington's ear.

Die Indicators: Obverse none observed

Reverse none observed

Description: Doubling shows as an extra tree branch to the right of the tree whose top lines up with the top right point of the state outline.

Die Indicators: Obverse A die chip shows on the base of Washington's neck left of the designers' initials. A die break appears on top of the designer's initials JF.

Reverse none observed

KENC 25¢ 2005 P MN DDR-003

Description: Doubling shows as parts of an extra tree near the bottom right of the tree whose top lines up with the top right point of the state outline.

Die Indicators: Obverse none observed

                 Reverse none observed

KENC 25¢ 2005 P MN DDR-004

Description: Doubling shows as part of an extra tree to the right of the tree whose top lines up with the top right point of the state outline.

Die Indicators: Obverse A long die crack starts left of and goes through the base of Washington's neck. Die chips appear on the top of the designer's initials JF.

                 Reverse none observed

Description: Doubling shows as an extra tree, right of the tree whose top lines up with the top right point of the state outline.

Die Indicators: Obverse none observed

Reverse none observed

2005 Oregon

Area(s) of Interest:

Below Washington's ear

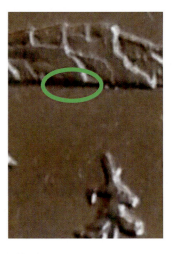

At the shoreline in the distance

Below the long upper right branch of the tall pine tree

Below the island in the lake

KENC 25¢ 2005 P OR DDO-001

Description: Close doubling shows below Washington's ear.

Die Indicators: Obverse none observed

                      Reverse none observed

KENC 25¢ 2005 P OR DDR-001

Description: Doubling shows at the shoreline in the distance.

Die Indicators: Obverse none observed

                      Reverse none observed

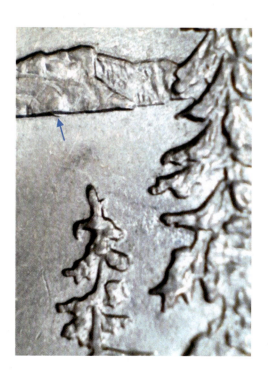

Description: Doubling shows below the long upper right branch of the tall pine tree.

Die Indicators: Obverse none observed

Reverse none observed

Description: Strong doubling shows below the island in the lake.

Die Indicators: Obverse none observed

Reverse none observed

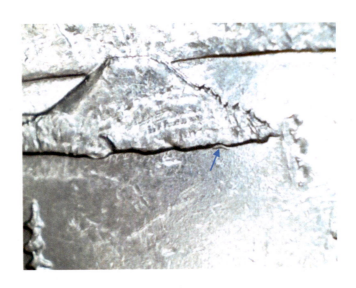

2005 West Virginia

Area(s) of Interest:

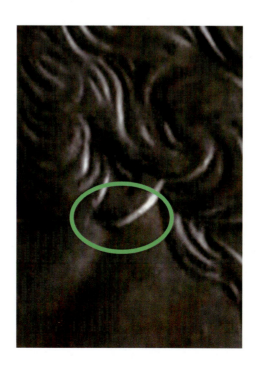

Below Washington's ear

Description: Doubling shows below Washington's ear.

Die Indicators: Obverse A die crack runs through the designer's initials JF.

Reverse none observed

2006 Nebraska

Area(s) of Interest:

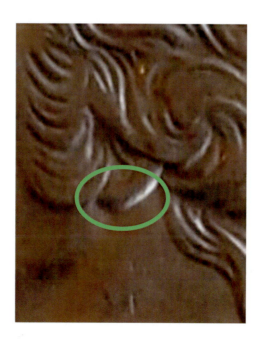

Below Washington's ear

Description: Doubling shows below Washington's ear.

Die Indicators: Obverse none observed

Reverse none observed

2006 Colorado

Area(s) of Interest:

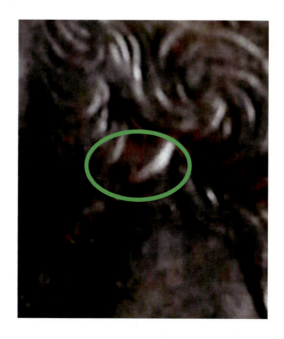

Below Washington's ear

Description: Doubling shows below Washington's ear.

Die Indicators: Obverse none observed

Reverse none observed

2006 North Dakota

Area(s) of Interest:

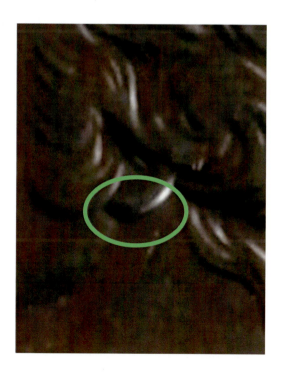

Below Washington's ear

Description: Doubling shows below Washington's ear.

Die Indicators: Obverse A die crack runs through the designer's initials JF.

Reverse none observed

2006 South Dakota

Area(s) of Interest:

Below Washington's ear

Description: Close doubling appears below Washington's ear.

Die Indicators: Obverse none observed

Reverse none observed

2007 Montana

Area(s) of Interest:

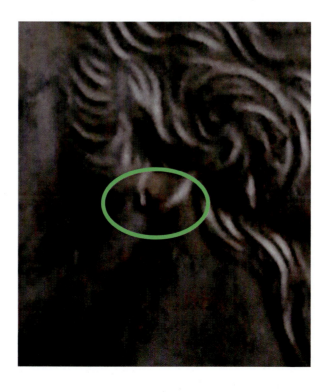

Below Washington's ear

KENC 25¢ 2007 P MT DDO-001

Description: Doubling shows below Washington's ear.

Die Indicators: Obverse none observed

Reverse none observed

KENC 25¢ 2007 P MT DDO-002

Description: Strong doubling shows below Washington's ear.

Die Indicators: Obverse none observed

Reverse none observed

2007 Washington

Area(s) of Interest:

Below Washington's ear

Description: Doubling shows below Washington's ear.

Die Indicators: Obverse A die break appears on the base of Washington's neck. A die crack runs through the base of Washington's neck, traveling through the designers' initials JF, WC.

Reverse none observed

2007 Idaho

Area(s) of Interest:

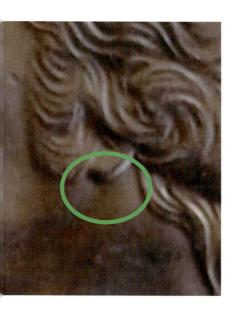

Below Washington's ear

The right arm of the star

The top left of the state outline

Description: Doubling shows below Washington's ear.

Die Indicators: Obverse none observed

Reverse none observed

Description: Doubling shows inside the right arm of the star in the state outline.

Die Indicators: Obverse none observed

Reverse none observed

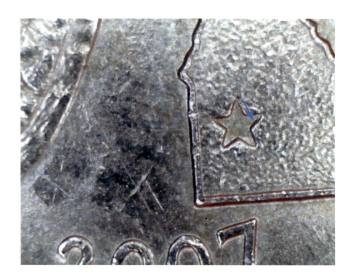

Description: Doubling at an angle shows along the top left of the state outline.

Die Indicators: Obverse A die crack and die chips appear on the designers' initials JF, WC.

Reverse A die chip appears in the left arm of the star in the state outline.

2007 Wyoming

Area(s) of Interest:

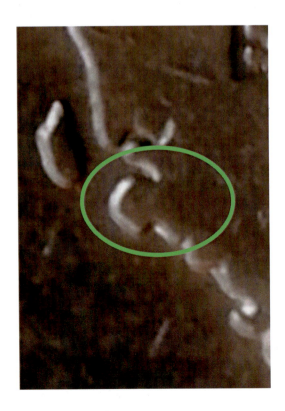

**Around the saddle horn and along
the horse's mane**

Description: Doubling shows along the lower portion of the saddle horn.

Die Indicators: Obverse none observed

Reverse none observed

Description: Doubling shows along the saddle horn.

Die Indicators: Obverse none observed

Reverse none observed

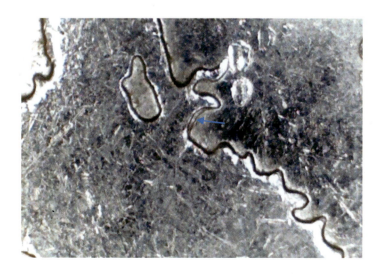

KENC 25¢ 2007 P WY DDR-003

Description: Doubling shows below the top of the saddle horn and just behind the horse's mane.

Die Indicators: Obverse none observed

Reverse none observed

KENC 25¢ 2007 P WY DDR-004

Description: Close, thin doubling shows just below the top of the saddle horn.

Die Indicators: Obverse none observed

Reverse none observed

Description: Doubling shows along the lower portion of the saddle horn. This is similar to *KENC 25¢ 2007 P WY DDR-001*, but the doubling here is thinner.

Die Indicators: Obverse none observed

                    Reverse none observed

KENC 25¢ 2007 P WY DDR-006

Description: Doubling shows along the horse's mane.

Die Indicators: Obverse none observed

                    Reverse none observed

Description: Doubling shows along the back of the horse's neck and mane.

Die Indicators: Obverse none observed

 Reverse none observed

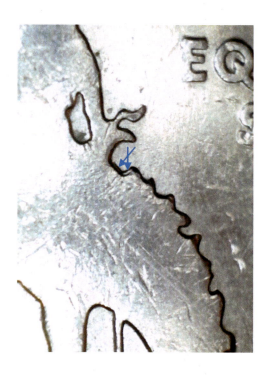

Description: Doubling travels along the saddle horn to the back of the horse's neck, and then goes over the beginning of the horse's mane.

Die Indicators: Obverse none observed

 Reverse none observed

Description: Strong doubling shows along the lower part of the saddle horn and along the back of the horse's neck.

Die Indicators: Obverse none observed

Reverse none observed

Description: Doubling shows as an extra lock of hair from the horse's mane.

Die Indicators: Obverse A die chip fills the opening of the R in TRUST. Die chips appear on the designers' initials JF, WC.

Reverse none observed

Description: Doubling shows along the back of the horse's neck and mane.

Die Indicators: Obverse none observed

Reverse none observed

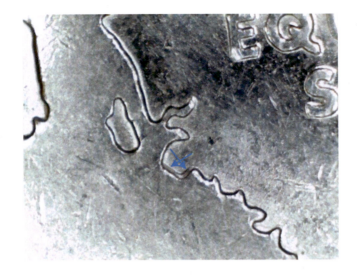

2007 Utah

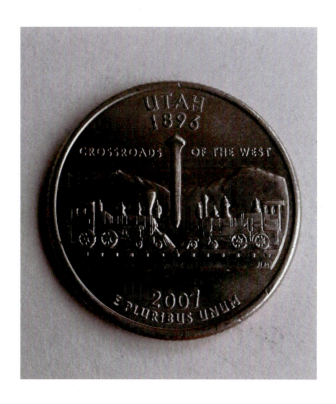

Area(s) of Interest:

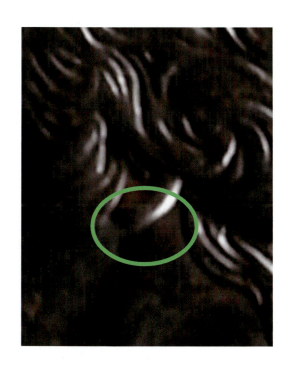

Below Washington's ear

Along the left side of the railroad spike

KENC 25¢ 2007 P UT DDO-001

Description: Doubling shows below Washington's ear.

Die Indicators: Obverse none observed

> Reverse A die break shows on the train that is to the right of the railroad spike.

KENC 25¢ 2007 P UT DDO-002/DDR-004

Description: Close doubling shows below Washington's ear. Doubling also shows along the lower left side of the railroad spike.

Die Indicators: Obverse A long die crack starts just left of, and then runs through the base of Washington's neck.

> Reverse A die chip appears on the 6 of 1896.

 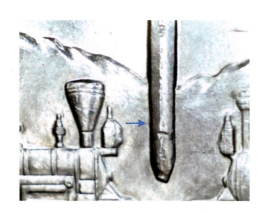  

KENC 25¢ 2007 P UT DDR-001

Description: Doubling shows along the lower left side of the railroad spike.

Die Indicators: Obverse none observed

Reverse none observed

KENC 25¢ 2007 P UT DDR-002

Description: Doubling shows along the lower left side of the railroad spike.

Die Indicators: Obverse none observed

Reverse none observed

Description: Close doubling at a slight angle shows along the left side of the railroad spike.

Die Indicators: Obverse none observed

Reverse none observed

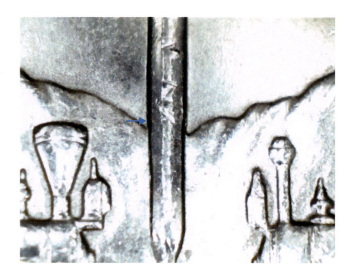

Description: Minor doubling shows along the lower left side of the railroad spike.

Die Indicators: Obverse none observed

Reverse none observed

2008 New Mexico

Area(s) of Interest:

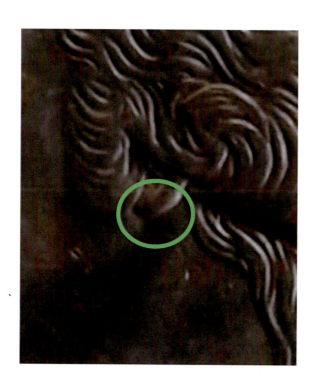 

Below Washington's ear

The lower rays

KENC 25¢ 2008 P NM DDO-001

Description: Doubling shows below Washington's ear.

Die Indicators: Obverse none observed

Reverse A die chip shows on the top right of the state outline.

KENC 25¢ 2008 P NM DDO-002

Description: Doubling shows below Washington's ear.

Die Indicators: Obverse none observed

Reverse none observed

KENC 25¢ 2008 P NM DDR-001

Description: Doubling shows along the right side of the lower central left ray.

Die Indicators: Obverse A die chip appears in the lower opening of the B in LIBERTY.

Reverse none observed

KENC 25¢ 2008 P NM DDR-002

Description: Doubling shows along the left side of the lower central left ray.

Die Indicators: Obverse A die chip appears between the designers' initials JF, WC.

Reverse none observed

2008 Arizona

Area(s) of Interest:

Below Washington's ear

Description: Doubling shows below Washington's ear.

Die Indicators: Obverse A long die crack starts left of and goes through the base of Washington's neck.

Reverse none observed

2008 Alaska

Area(s) of Interest:

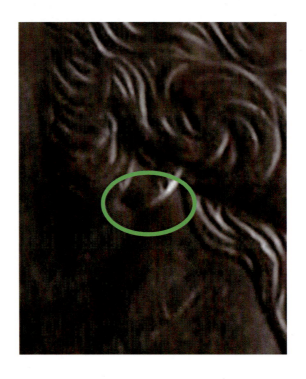

Around Washington's lower ear

Description: Doubling curves around the back of Washington's ear.

Die Indicators: Obverse none observed

Reverse A die chip appears between the bear's claws.

2008 Hawaii

Area(s) of Interest:

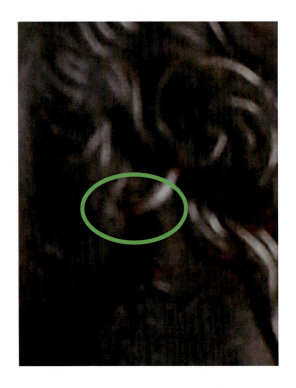

Around Washington's lower ear

Description: Doubling curves around the back of Washington's ear.

Die Indicators: Obverse none observed

Reverse none observed

2009 District of Columbia

Area(s) of Interest:

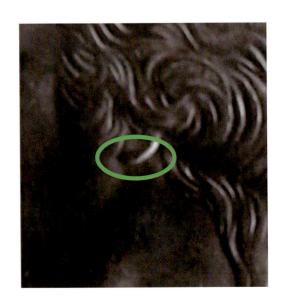

Below Washington's ear

The piano keys below the E in ELLINGTON and along Duke Ellington's elbow

Description: Doubling shows below Washington's ear.

Die Indicators: Obverse none observed

Reverse none observed

Description: Doubling shows below Washington's ear.

Die Indicators: Obverse none observed

Reverse none observed

KENC 25¢ 2009 P DC DDR-001

Description: Doubling shows as an extra black piano key below the E in ELLINGTON.

Die Indicators: Obverse none observed

Reverse none observed

KENC 25¢ 2009 P DC DDR-002

Description: Doubling shows along the side of Duke Ellington's elbow.

Die Indicators: Obverse none observed

Reverse none observed

2009 Puerto Rico

Area(s) of Interest:

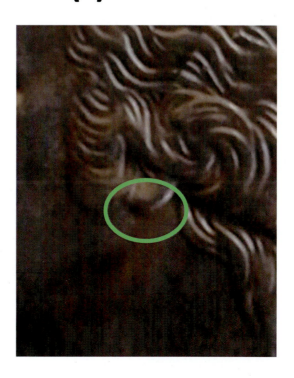

Below Washington's ear

Description: Doubling shows below Washington's ear.

Die Indicators: Obverse none observed

Reverse none observed

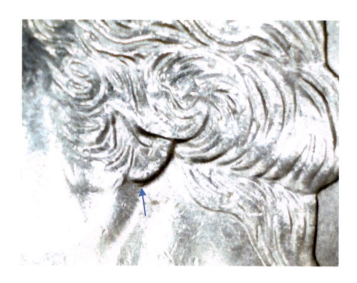

Description: Doubling shows below Washington's ear.

Die Indicators: Obverse A long heavy die crack runs through the base of Washington's neck and through the designers' initials JF, WC.

Reverse none observed

2012 Hawaii Hawai'i Volcanoes

Area(s) of Interest:

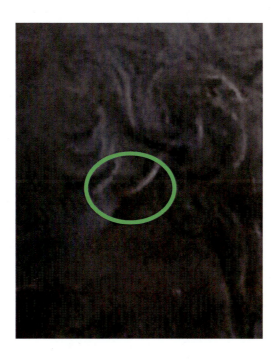

Below Washington's ear

KENC 25¢ 2012 P HI DDO-001

Description: Doubling shows below Washington's ear.

Die Indicators: Obverse none observed

       Reverse A die chip appears near the top of the lava erupting out of the volcano.

KENC 25¢ 2012 P HI DDO-002

Description: Doubling shows below Washington's ear.

Die Indicators: Obverse none observed

       Reverse A die chip appears near the top of the lava erupting out of the volcano.

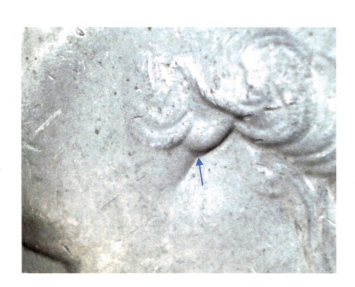 

2012 Puerto Rico El Yunque

Area(s) of Interest:

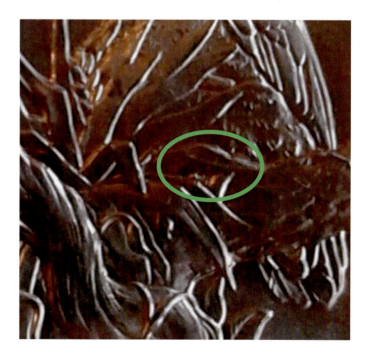

The leaf above the parrot's foot

Description: Doubling shows underneath the leaf above the parrot's foot.

Die Indicators: Obverse none observed

                       Reverse none observed

2012 Alaska Denali

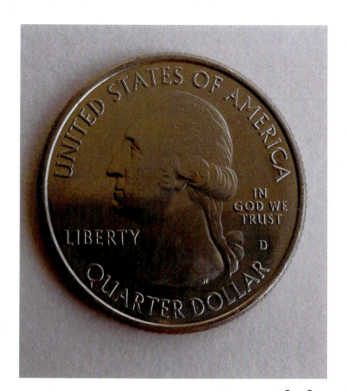 

Area(s) of Interest:

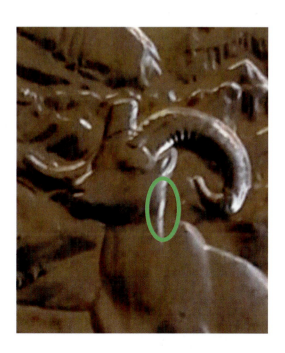

Behind the sheep's neck

KENC 25¢ 2012 P AK DDR-001

Description: Doubling shows behind the sheep's neck.

Die Indicators: *Obverse* none observed

Reverse none observed

KENC 25¢ 2012 P AK DDR-002

Description: Thick doubling shows behind the sheep's neck.

Die Indicators: *Obverse* A die crack with a die chip at its center appears left of the designer's initials JF.

Reverse none observed

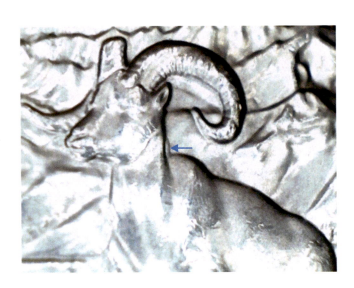 

Description: Doubling shows behind the sheep's neck.

Die Indicators: Obverse none observed

Reverse none observed

2013 New Hampshire White Mountain

Area(s) of Interest:

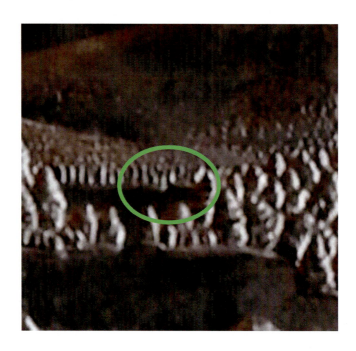

Around the trees and at the shoreline

Description: Doubling shows as extra parts of a tree appearing in the lake. Doubling also appears on the shoreline of the lake.

Die Indicators: Obverse none observed

Reverse none observed

2013 Ohio Perry's Victory

Area(s) of Interest:

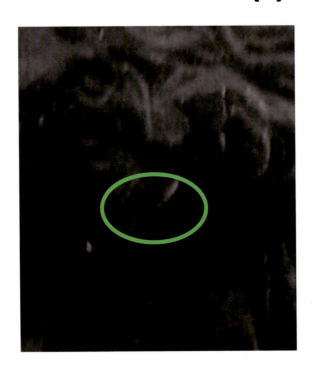
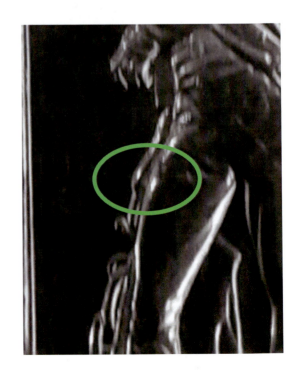

Below and behind Washington's ear

Perry's coat and outer thigh

KENC 25¢ 2013 P OH DDO-001

Description: Strong doubling shows below Washington's ear.

Die Indicators: Obverse none observed

Reverse none observed

KENC 25¢ 2013 P OH DDO-002

Description: Doubling shows behind Washington's ear.

Die Indicators: Obverse none observed

Reverse none observed

Description: Strong doubling shows below Washington's ear.

Die Indicators: Obverse none observed

                       Reverse none observed

KENC 25¢ 2013 P OH DDO-004

Description: Strong doubling shows below Washington's ear. This is extremely similar to *KENC 25¢ 2013 P OH DDO-003*, but the bottom of the doubling here is slightly thicker and dips further below the ear.

Die Indicators: Obverse none observed

                       Reverse none observed

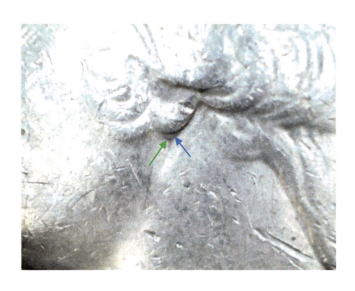

Description: Close doubling shows on Perry's coat and outer thigh.

Die Indicators: Obverse none observed

Reverse none observed

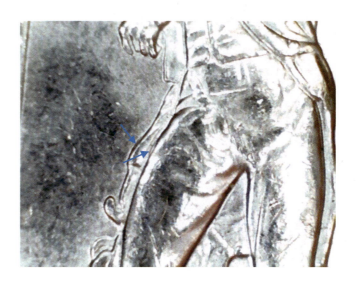

KENC 25¢ 2013 P OH DDR-002

Description: Strong doubling can be seen on Perry's coat.

Die Indicators: Obverse none observed

Reverse none observed

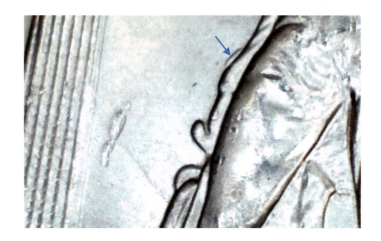

Description: Very close doubling shows on Perry's coat.

Die Indicators: Obverse none observed

                        Reverse none observed

2013 Nevada Great Basin

Area(s) of Interest:

Lower left branch

Leaves near the upper openings between branches

Leaves above the lower right branch, Lower right branch and leaves, Central trunk location

Right side of the trunk, Lower right roots, Rocks beneath the tree

Bottom roots, Rocks beneath the tree

Description: Doubling shows along the top leaves of the tree's lower right branch.

Die Indicators: Obverse none observed

                         Reverse none observed

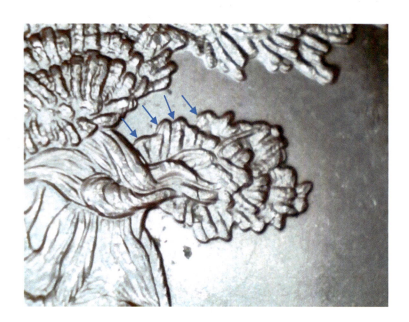

Description: Doubling shows along the tree's lower left root, lower left branch, leaves near the upper openings between branches, lower right branch and leaves, lower right roots, bottom roots, and central trunk location. Doubling also shows along the tops of the rocks beneath the tree.

Die Indicators: Obverse none observed

Reverse none observed

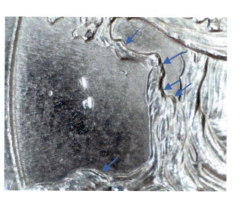
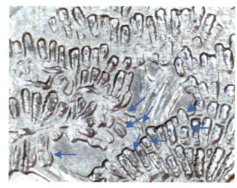

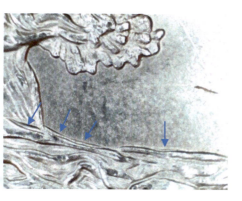
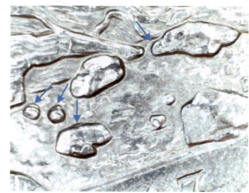
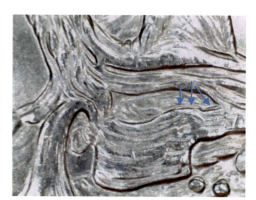

Description: Doubling shows along the tree's lower left branch, leaves near the upper openings between branches, leaves above the lower right branch, right side of the trunk, bottom roots, and central trunk location.

Die Indicators: Obverse none observed

Reverse none observed

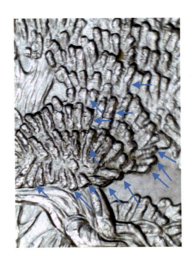

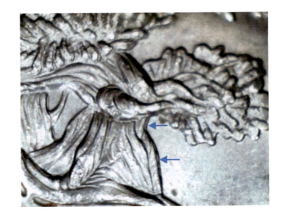

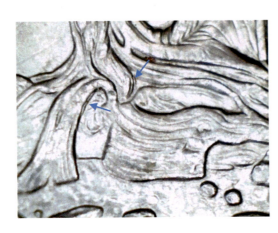

Description: Doubling shows along the tree's lower left branch. Doubling shows on top of the rocks beneath the tree.

Die Indicators: Obverse none observed

Reverse A die chip appears at the edge of the tree's upper right branch.

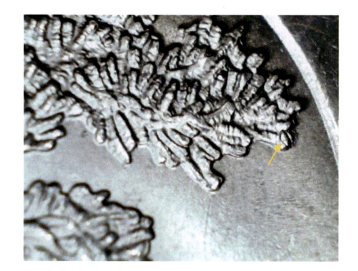

Description: Doubling shows along the tree's lower left branch, leaves near the upper openings between branches, leaves above the lower right branch, lower right branch and leaves, right side of the trunk, bottom roots, and central trunk location. Doubling also shows along the rocks beneath the tree.

Die Indicators: Obverse none observed

                      Reverse none observed

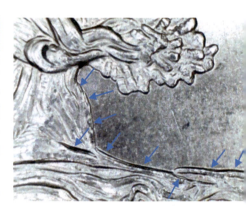

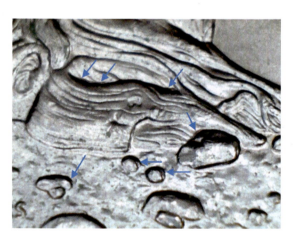

Description: Doubling shows along the tree's lower right branch leaves, lower right roots, and bottom roots. Doubling also shows along the tops of the rocks beneath the tree.

Die Indicators: Obverse none observed

Reverse none observed

 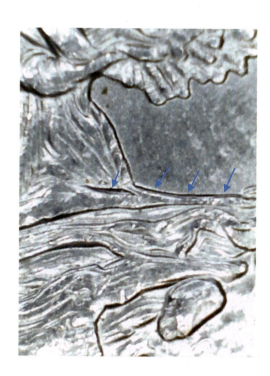

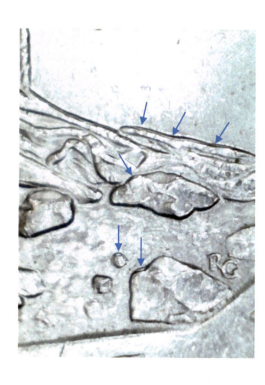 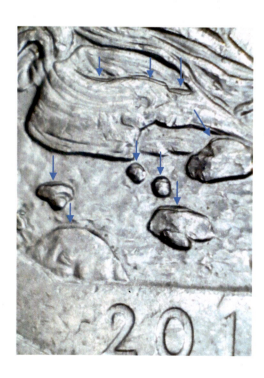

2013 Maryland Fort McHenry

Area(s) of Interest:

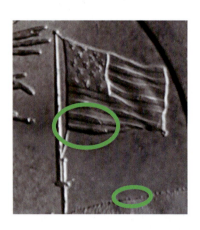

The USA Flag (particularly the lower stripes and below the bottom stripe) and rooftop below

The upper and lower firework bursts

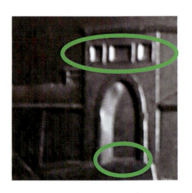

The three windows, the archway (particularly at the bottom of the archway), and the rooftop above the windows

The rooftops, along the wall of the right building

Description: Doubling shows as heavy extra thickness on the USA Flag, firework bursts, rooftops, windows, and archway. Doubling also shows as an extra streak from the upper firework burst, just left of the top of the flagpole.

Die Indicators: Obverse none observed

Reverse none observed

 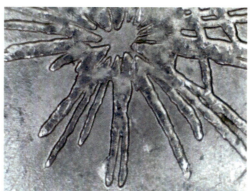 

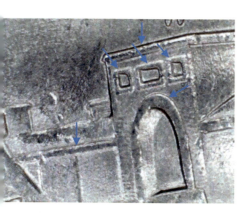  

KENC 25¢ 2013 P MD DDR-002

Description: Doubling shows above the roof of the middle building.

Die Indicators: Obverse none observed

Reverse none observed

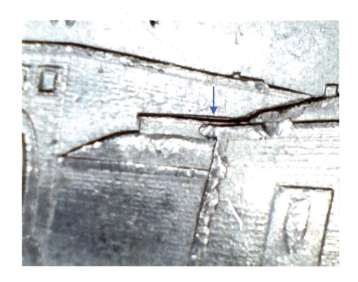

KENC 25¢ 2013 P MD DDR-003

Description: Doubling shows along the bottom stripes of the USA Flag. Doubling shows within the upper firework burst.

Die Indicators: Obverse none observed

Reverse none observed

 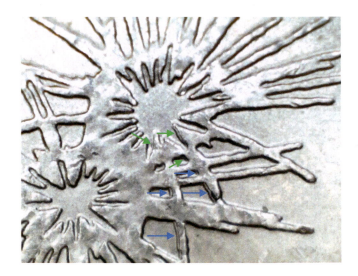

Description: Doubling shows along the bottom stripes of the USA Flag, the rooftops of the middle and right buildings, and along the wall of the right building.

Die Indicators: Obverse none observed

　　　　　　　　　　Reverse none observed

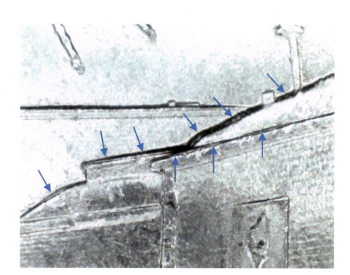

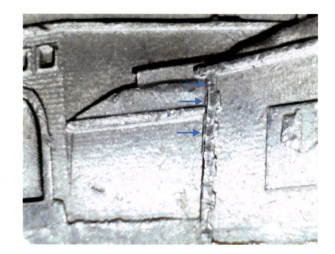

Description: Doubling shows along the bottom stripe of the USA Flag, the rooftops of the middle and right buildings, and along the wall of the right building. This is extremely similar to *KENC 25¢ 2013 P MD DDR-004*, but only the bottom stripe of the USA Flag shows doubling. Also, there is additional doubling on top of the right building's roof.

Die Indicators: Obverse none observed

Reverse none observed

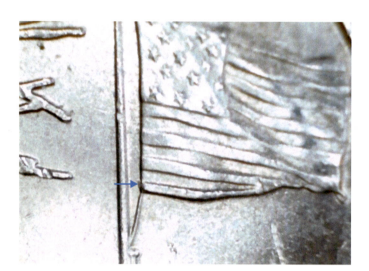
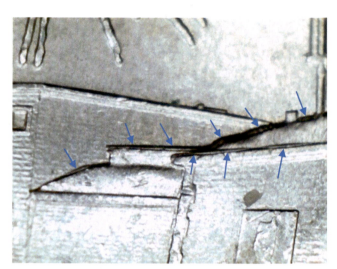

Description: Doubling shows along the bottoms of the middle and right windows, at the bottom of the archway, and above the rooftops. The doubling above the roof of the middle building is very strong.

Die Indicators: Obverse none observed

Reverse none observed

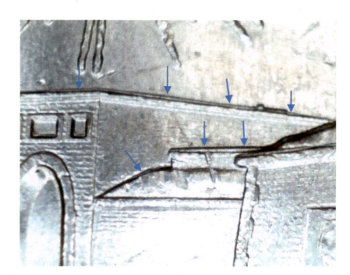

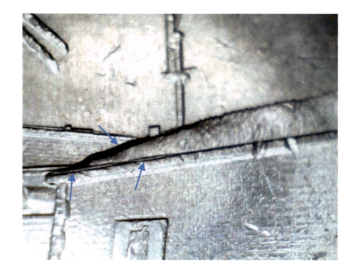

Description: Doubling shows along the bottom stripes of the USA Flag. Doubling shows within the upper firework burst. This is similar to *KENC 25¢ 2013 P MD DDR-003*, but there is no doubling inside the center of the upper firework burst.

Die Indicators: Obverse none observed

Reverse none observed

Description: Doubling shows along the bottoms of the three windows, at the bottom of the archway, and above the rooftops.

Die Indicators: Obverse none observed

Reverse none observed

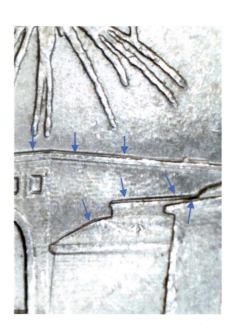

Description: Doubling shows as heavy extra thickness on the USA Flag, firework bursts, rooftops, windows, and archway. This is extremely similar to *KENC 25¢ 2013 P MD DDR-001*, but there is no extra streak from the upper firework burst.

Die Indicators: Obverse none observed

Reverse none observed

Description: Strong doubling shows along the bottom of the USA Flag. Doubling shows along the lower and upper firework bursts.

Die Indicators: Obverse none observed

Reverse none observed

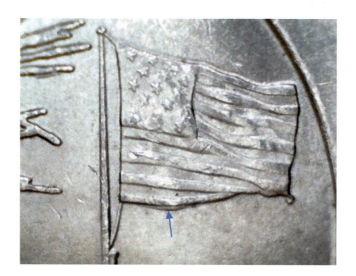

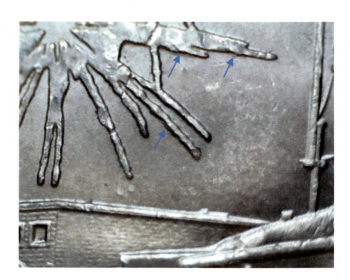

2013 South Dakota Mount Rushmore

Area(s) of Interest:

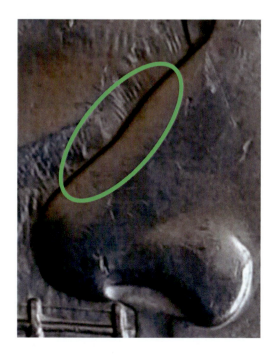

Along Jefferson's nose

Description: Doubling shows along the bridge of Jefferson's nose.

Die Indicators: Obverse none observed

Reverse none observed

KENC 25¢ 2013 P SD DDR-002

Description: Strong doubling shows along the bridge of Jefferson's nose.

Die Indicators: Obverse none observed

Reverse none observed

Description: Doubling shows along the bridge of Jefferson's nose.

Die Indicators: Obverse none observed

Reverse none observed

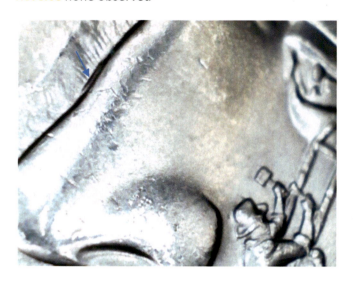 

KENC 25¢ 2013 P SD DDR-004

Description: Doubling shows along the bridge of Jefferson's nose.

Die Indicators: Obverse A die chip is at the beginning of a die crack which starts left of and then goes through the designer's initials JF.

Reverse A die crack extends northwest from the right side of the sculptor's foot.

KENC 25¢ 2013 P SD DDR-005

Description: Short, thick doubling shows along the bridge of Jefferson's nose.

Die Indicators: Obverse none observed

Reverse none observed

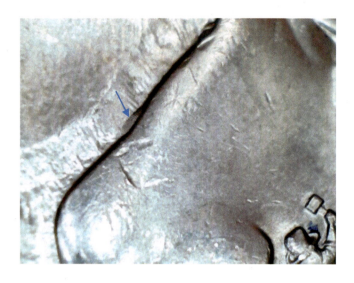 

KENC 25¢ 2013 P SD DDR-006

Description: Thick doubling shows along the bridge of Jefferson's nose.

Die Indicators: Obverse none observed

Reverse none observed

KENC 25¢ 2013 P SD DDR-007

Description: Strong doubling shows along the bridge of Jefferson's nose.

Die Indicators: Obverse A die crack and die chips are found above and to the right of the designer's initials JF.

Reverse A long die crack extends northwest from the right side of the sculptor's foot.

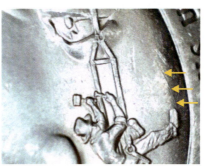

KENC 25¢ 2013 P SD DDR-008

Description: Doubling shows along the bridge of Jefferson's nose. This is extremely similar to *KENC 25¢ 2013 P SD DDR-002*, but the doubling here is thinner.

Die Indicators: Obverse none observed

Reverse A large die break appears below the S in RUSHMORE. Die chips and a die crack appear to the right of the sculptor's foot.

KENC 25¢ 2013 P SD DDR-009

Description: Doubling shows along the bridge of Jefferson's nose. This is similar to *KENC 25¢ 2013 P SD DDR-006*, but the doubling here is thinner. The bottom of the doubling is also more pointed rather than rounded back towards the nose.

Die Indicators: Obverse A die crack runs through the bottoms of the designer's initials JF.

Reverse none observed

KENC 25¢ 2013 P SD DDR-010

Description: Minor doubling shows on the bridge of Jefferson's nose.

Die Indicators: Obverse none observed

Reverse none observed

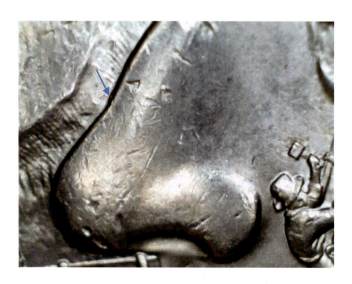

KENC 25¢ 2013 P SD DDR-011

Description: Close doubling shows along the bridge of Jefferson's nose.

Die Indicators: Obverse none observed

Reverse none observed

KENC 25¢ 2013 P SD DDR-012

Description: Long, thin doubling shows along the bridge of Jefferson's nose.

Die Indicators: Obverse none observed

Reverse none observed

KENC 25¢ 2013 P SD DDR-013

Description: Strong doubling shows along the bridge of Jefferson's nose. The doubling here is thinner than *KENC 25¢ 2013 P SD DDR-006*, but is not as long as nor pointed (the doubling here rounds back towards the nose) at the bottom like *KENC 25¢ 2013 P SD DDR-009*.

Die Indicators: Obverse none observed

Reverse none observed

KENC 25¢ 2013 P SD DDR-014

Description: A tiny amount of doubling can be found on the bridge of Jefferson's nose.

Die Indicators: Obverse none observed

Reverse none observed

KENC 25¢ 2013 P SD DDR-015

Description: Close doubling shows along the bridge of Jefferson's nose. This is similar to *KENC 25¢ 2013 P SD DDR-011*, but the doubling here is shorter and thinner.

Die Indicators: Obverse none observed

                         Reverse none observed

KENC 25¢ 2013 P SD DDR-016

Description: Close doubling shows along the bridge of Jefferson's nose. This is similar to *KENC 25¢ 2013 P SD DDR-011* and *KENC 25¢ 2013 P SD DDR-015*, but the doubling here is the thinnest and closest along the nose of the three.

Die Indicators: Obverse A die crack with a die chip at its center runs above the designer's initials JF.

                         Reverse A die crack runs from Jefferson's nose to the sculptor's hat.

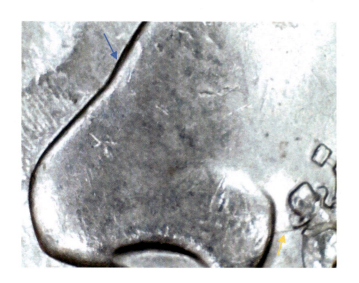
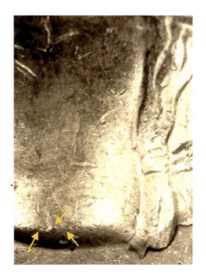

Description: Doubling shows along the bridge of Jefferson's nose. This is similar to *KENC 25¢ 2013 P SD DDR-008*, but the doubling here is shorter in length. The doubling here is also thicker at the bottom than *KENC 25¢ 2013 P SD DDR-008* is.

Die Indicators: Obverse none observed

Reverse none observed

KENC 25¢ 2013 P SD DDR-018

Description: Doubling shows along the bridge of Jefferson's nose. This is extremely similar to *KENC 25¢ 2013 P SD DDR-004*, but the doubling here is slightly thicker and slightly longer in length.

Die Indicators: Obverse none observed

Reverse A die crack runs north from the sculptor's foot.

Description: Doubling shows along the bridge of Jefferson's nose.

Die Indicators: Obverse none observed

Reverse none observed

 KENC 25¢ 2013 P SD DDR-020

Description: Strong, thick doubling shows along the bridge of Jefferson's nose. This is similar to *KENC 25¢ 2013 P SD DDR-006*, *KENC 25¢ 2013 P SD DDR-009*, and *KENC 25¢ 2013 P SD DDR-013*, but the doubling here clearly has the thickest bottom amongst the group.

Die Indicators: Obverse none observed

Reverse none observed

2014 Virginia Shenandoah

Area(s) of Interest:

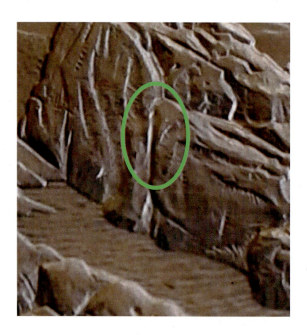

Along the edge of the large rock on the path

Description: Doubling shows along the large rock that appears on the path.

Die Indicators: Obverse none observed

Reverse none observed

2014 Utah Arches

Area(s) of Interest:

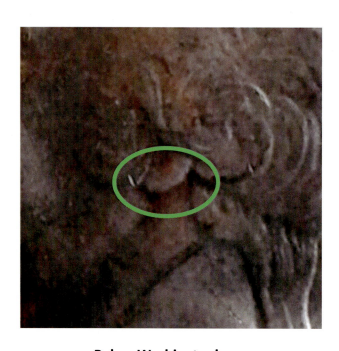

Below Washington's ear

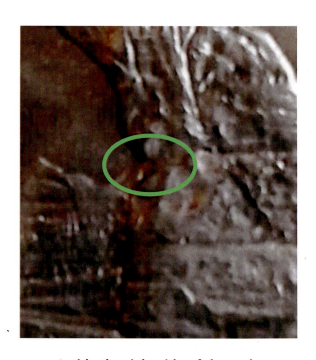

Inside the right side of the arch

Description: Strong doubling shows below Washington's ear.

Die Indicators: Obverse none observed

Reverse none observed

KENC 25¢ 2014 P UT DDR-001

Description: Strong doubling shows along the inside of the right side of the arch.

Die Indicators: Obverse none observed

Reverse none observed

KENC 25¢ 2014 P UT DDR-002

Description: Minor doubling shows along the inside of the right side of the arch.

Die Indicators: Obverse none observed

Reverse none observed

KENC 25¢ 2014 P UT DDR-003

Description: Doubling shows along the inside of the right side of the arch.

Die Indicators: Obverse none observed

Reverse none observed

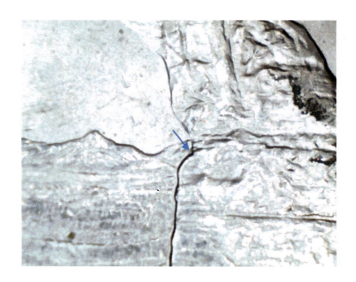

KENC 25¢ 2014 P UT DDR-004

Description: Doubling travels along the inside of the right side of the arch.

Die Indicators: Obverse none observed

Reverse none observed

KENC 25¢ 2014 P UT DDR-005

Description: Doubling shows along the inside of the right side of the arch.

Die Indicators: Obverse none observed

Reverse none observed

2015 Nebraska Homestead

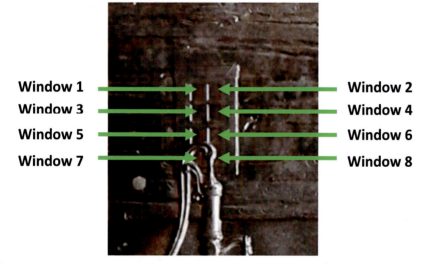

Window 1   Window 2

Window 3   Window 4

Window 5   Window 6

Window 7   Window 8

Area(s) of Interest:

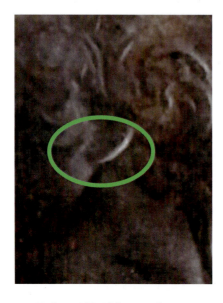

Below Washington's ear   Inside the windows and above the water pump

KENC 25¢ 2015 P NE DDO-001

Description: Doubling shows below Washington's earlobe.

Die Indicators: Obverse none observed

Reverse none observed

KENC 25¢ 2015 P NE DDR-001

Description: Doubling shows in the lower left side of window 4 and in the upper left corner of window 6. Doubling from the top of the water pump goes through the center of windows 5 and 6.

Die Indicators: Obverse none observed

Reverse none observed

KENC 25¢ 2015 P NE DDR-002

Description: Very close doubling shows in the upper right corner of window 3 and the upper portion of window 4.

Die Indicators: **Obverse** none observed

Reverse none observed

KENC 25¢ 2015 P NE DDR-003

Description: Very close doubling shows in the top center of window 6.

Die Indicators: **Obverse** none observed

Reverse A die break shows on the left side of the roof.

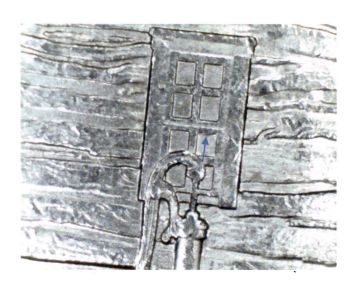 

Description: Doubling at a southeast angle shows in the top center of window 6.

Die Indicators: Obverse none observed

Reverse none observed

Description: Doubling shows along the right and bottom right of window 3.

Die Indicators: Obverse none observed

Reverse A forming die break depression shows on the left side of the roof.

KENC 25¢ 2015 P NE DDR-006

Description: Doubling shows along the center right side of window 6.

Die Indicators: **Obverse** none observed

Reverse none observed

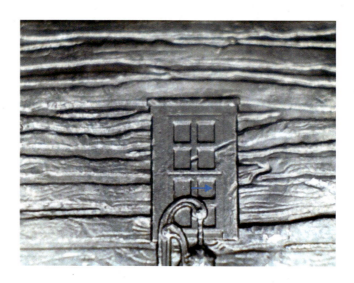

KENC 25¢ 2015 P NE DDR-007

Description: Doubling shows along the upper left side of window 5.

Die Indicators: **Obverse** none observed

Reverse none observed

Description: Strong doubling shows at the top of window 4.

Die Indicators: *Obverse* none observed

   Reverse A die chip shows on the left side of the roof.

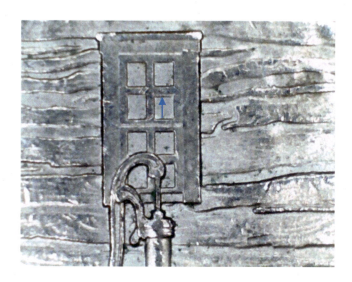 

Description: Doubling at a southeast angle shows in the top center of window 6. *This doubled die is similar to KENC 25¢ 2015 P NE DDR-004*, but the doubling is not as thick and slopes downward at a less sharp angle.

Die Indicators: *Obverse* none observed

   Reverse none observed

Description: Doubling shows along the right side and bottom of window 3.

Die Indicators: Obverse none observed

Reverse none observed

Description: Doubling appears in windows 3 and 4 near window 3's upper right corner and window 4's upper left corner.

Die Indicators: Obverse none observed

Reverse none observed

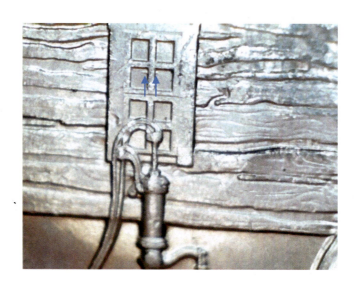

KENC 25¢ 2015 P NE DDR-012

Description: Doubling shows along the right side of window 3.

Die Indicators: Obverse none observed

Reverse none observed

KENC 25¢ 2015 P NE DDR-013

Description: Doubling at a slight angle shows along the left side of window 4.

Die Indicators: Obverse none observed

Reverse none observed

Description: Very close doubling shows in the bottom left corner of window 4.

Die Indicators: Obverse none observed

Reverse A die break appears on the left side of the roof.

KENC 25¢ 2015 P NE DDR-015

Description: Doubling shows along the top of window 6.

Die Indicators: Obverse none observed

Reverse A die chip shows on the top left leaf of the corn that is left of the homestead. A forming die break depression shows on the right side of the roof near the corn leaf.

KENC 25¢ 2015 P NE DDR-016

Description: Doubling travels around the top right corner of window 6.

Die Indicators: Obverse none observed

Reverse A long forming die break depression runs above the right side of the roof.

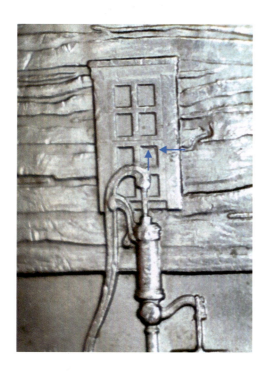

KENC 25¢ 2015 P NE DDR-017

Description: Doubling at sharp angles show in the lower half of window 4.

Die Indicators: Obverse none observed

Reverse A die chip is on the left side of the roof.

Description: Extremely close doubling shows in the bottom left of window 4.

Die Indicators: Obverse none observed

Reverse A die chip shows above the right side of the roof.

KENC 25¢ 2015 P NE DDR-019

Description: Doubling shows in the upper right of window 3.

Die Indicators: Obverse none observed

Reverse none observed

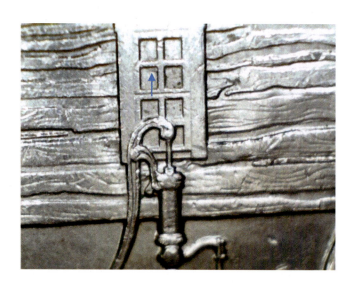

Description: Doubling travels around the top right corner of window 3.

Die Indicators: Obverse none observed

Reverse none observed

Description: Doubling shows along the top and right side of window 3.

Die Indicators: Obverse none observed

Reverse none observed

KENC 25¢ 2015 P NE DDR-022

Description: Strong doubling shows along the top and right side of window 4. Slight doubling also shows at the bottom of window 4.

Die Indicators: Obverse A die chip shows at the base of Washington's neck, left of the designer's initials JF.

Reverse A die chip shows between the husk and leaf of the corn to the left of the homestead. Die breaks appear on both the left and right sides of the roof.

KENC 25¢ 2015 P NE DDR-023

Description: Doubling goes across and up through window 3, and appears near the bottom right corner of window 1.

Die Indicators: Obverse none observed

Reverse A die chip appears above the left side of the roof.

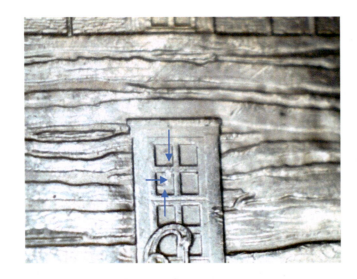

KENC 25¢ 2015 P NE DDR-024

Description: Doubling shows above the water pump near the bottom right of window 5 and bottom left of window 6. There is also doubling in the bottom right corner of window 6.

Die Indicators: Obverse none observed

Reverse A die chip appears above the left side of the roof. A die chip and forming die break depression show above the right side of the roof.

KENC 25¢ 2015 P NE DDR-025

Description: Doubling shows along the left side and in the top left corner of window 4.

Die Indicators: Obverse none observed

Reverse A die chip shows on the left side of the corn left of the homestead.

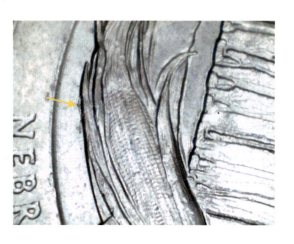

KENC 25¢ 2015 P NE DDR-026

Description: Strong doubling at a downward slope appears at the bottom of window 4.

Die Indicators: Obverse none observed

Reverse A die chip shows on the left side of the roof.

KENC 25¢ 2015 P NE DDR-027

Description: Doubling shows near the bottom right corner of window 3.

Die Indicators: Obverse Die chips appear on the base of Washington's neck, left of the designer's initials JF.

Reverse A very large forming die break depression shows above the right side of the roof.

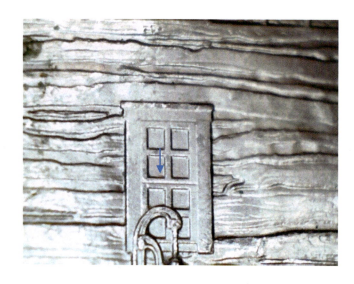
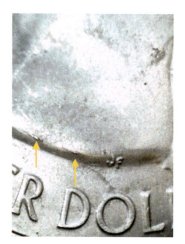

KENC 25¢ 2015 P NE DDR-028

Description: Strong doubling shows above the water pump.

Die Indicators: Obverse none observed

Reverse none observed

KENC 25¢ 2015 P NE DDR-029

Description: Doubling at a slight southwest angle shows at the top of window 5.

Die Indicators: Obverse none observed

Reverse A forming die break depression shows above the right side of the roof.

Description: Light doubling from the water pump shows inside window 5.

Die Indicators: Obverse none observed

Reverse A die chip shows above the right side of the roof.

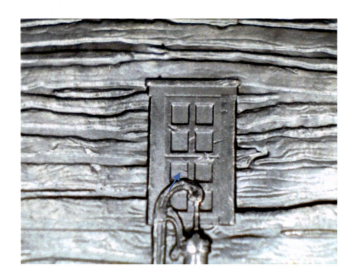 

2015 North Carolina Blue Ridge Parkway

Area(s) of Interest:

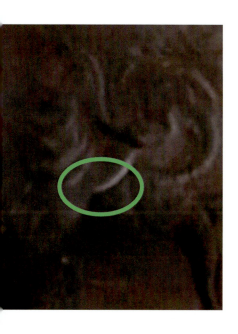 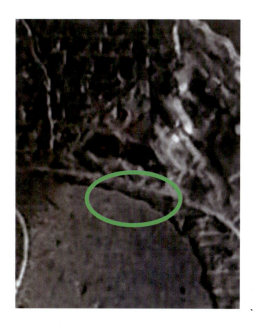 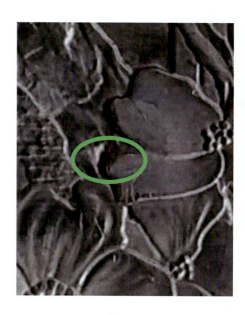

elow and behind Washington's ear

Along the ridge of the road

Upper left of the top flower's bottom petal

Description: Doubling shows below and behind Washington's ear.

Die Indicators: Obverse none observed

Reverse A die chip and forming die break depression show to the right of the top flower's top petal.

KENC 25¢ 2015 P NC DDO-002

Description: Doubling shows below Washington's ear.

Die Indicators: Obverse none observed

Reverse none observed

Description: Doubling shows along the ridge of the road.

Die Indicators: Obverse none observed

Reverse none observed

Description: Very close doubling shows along the ridge of the road.

Die Indicators: Obverse none observed

Reverse none observed

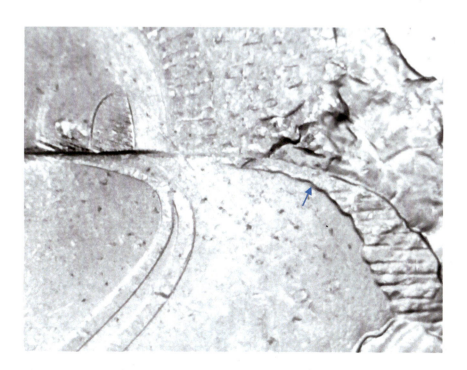

Description: Minor doubling shows along the ridge of the road.

Die Indicators: Obverse none observed

Reverse none observed

Description: Close doubling shows along the ridge of the road.

Die Indicators: Obverse none observed

Reverse none observed

KENC 25¢ 2015 P NC DDR-005

Description: Doubling shows along the ridge of the road. This is similar to *KENC 25¢ 2015 P NC DDR-002*, but the doubling here curves left into the road at its top.

Die Indicators: Obverse none observed

Reverse none observed

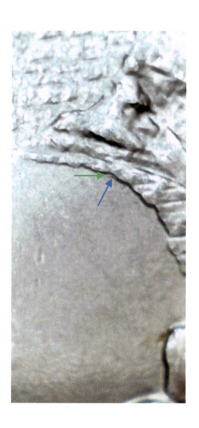

KENC 25¢ 2015 P NC DDR-006

Description: Doubling shows along the upper left of the top flower's bottom petal.

Die Indicators: Obverse none observed

Reverse none observed

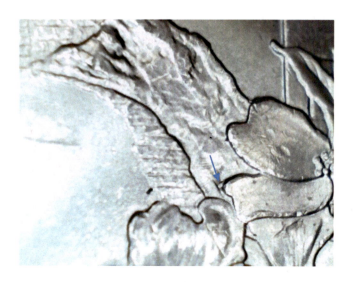

2015 Delaware Bombay Hook

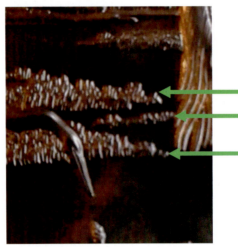

Upper marsh strip

Middle marsh strip

Lower marsh strip

Area(s) of Interest:

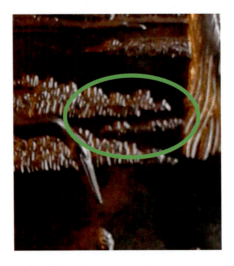

The marsh strips between the two water birds

Description: Doubling shows above the center of the middle marsh strip.

Die Indicators: Obverse none observed

Reverse none observed

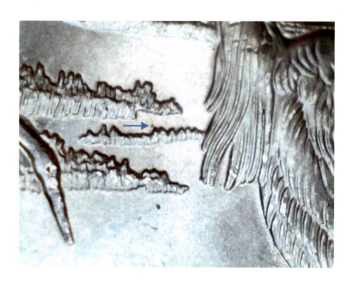

Description: Doubling shows underneath the right side of the upper marsh strip.

Die Indicators: Obverse none observed

Reverse none observed

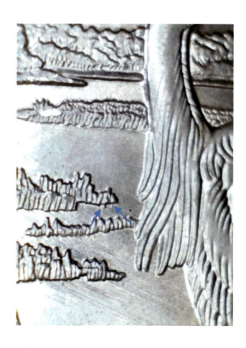

KENC 25¢ 2015 P DE DDR-003

Description: Doubling shows at the top of the middle marsh strip.

Die Indicators: Obverse none observed

Reverse Die chips appear around the heron's beak.

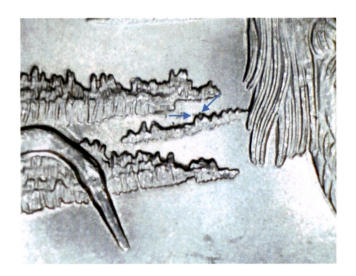 

KENC 25¢ 2015 P DE DDR-004

Description: Extreme doubling appears above the middle marsh strip.

Die Indicators: Obverse Die chips and a die crack appear on and around the designer's initials JF.

Reverse none observed

Description: Doubling appears above the right side of the upper marsh strip.

Die Indicators: Obverse none observed

Reverse A large die chip appears near the heron's beak.

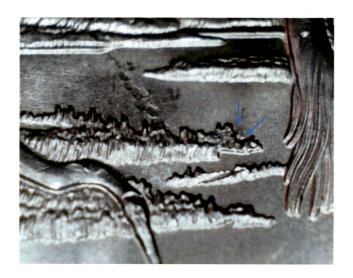 

Description: Very close doubling appears underneath the right side of the upper marsh strip.

Die Indicators: Obverse none observed

Reverse Die chips appear around the heron's beak.

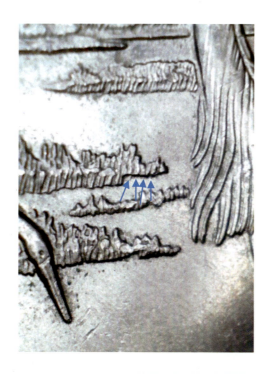 

Description: Doubling appears underneath the right side of the upper marsh strip.

Die Indicators: Obverse none observed

   Reverse A large die chip appears near the heron's beak.

Description: Doubling appears underneath the right side of the upper marsh strip.

Die Indicators: Obverse none observed

   Reverse none observed

KENC 25¢ 2015 P DE DDR-009

Description: Doubling appears underneath the right side of the upper marsh strip.

Die Indicators: Obverse none observed

Reverse none observed

KENC 25¢ 2015 P DE DDR-010

Description: Doubling appears at the top of the middle marsh strip.

Die Indicators: Obverse A die chip appears northwest of the designer's initials JF.

Reverse A die chip appears near the heron's beak.

Description: Close doubling appears underneath the right side of the upper marsh strip.

Die Indicators: Obverse none observed

Reverse A long die chip appears near the heron's beak.

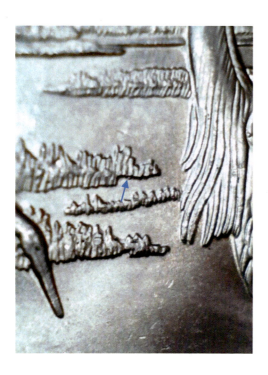

KENC 25¢ 2015 P DE DDR-012

Description: Doubling appears below the right side of the upper marsh strip. The bottom left of the doubling is pointed.

Die Indicators: Obverse none observed

Reverse Die chips appear around the heron's beak.

Description: Doubling appears on top of the left side of the middle marsh strip.

Die Indicators: Obverse A die chip appears northeast of the designer's initials JF.

Reverse A die chip appears below the heron's eye.

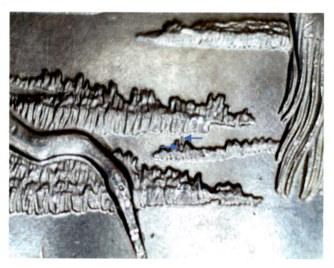  

Description: Doubling appears underneath the right side of the upper marsh strip.

Die Indicators: Obverse none observed

Reverse none observed

Description: Doubling at an angle appears at the top of the middle marsh strip.

Die Indicators: Obverse none observed

Reverse Die chips appear around the heron's beak.

KENC 25¢ 2015 P DE DDR-016

Description: Doubling appears below the right side of the upper marsh strip. This is similar to *KENC 25¢ 2015 P DE DDR-012*, but the doubling here is smaller in size and rounded at the bottom.

Die Indicators: Obverse A die chip appears on the designer's initials JF.

Reverse none observed

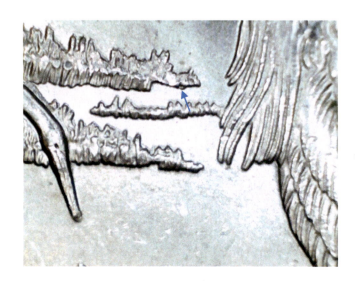 

KENC 25¢ 2015 P DE DDR-017

Description: Scattered doubling appears above and below the middle marsh strip.

Die Indicators: Obverse none observed

Reverse none observed

KENC 25¢ 2015 P DE DDR-018

Description: Doubling appears at the center of the middle marsh strip.

Die Indicators: Obverse none observed

Reverse none observed

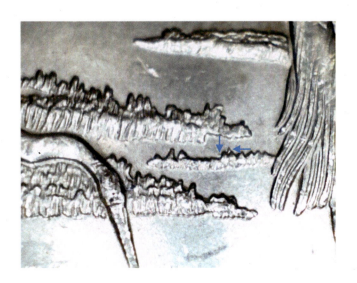

Description: Strong doubling appears above the right side of the upper marsh strip.

Die Indicators: Obverse none observed

Reverse none observed

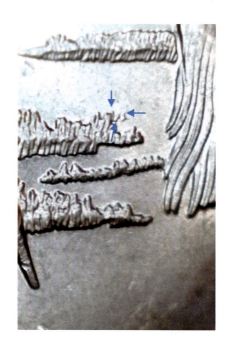

Description: Doubling appears underneath the right side of the upper marsh strip.

Die Indicators: Obverse none observed

Reverse none observed

KENC 25¢ 2015 P DE DDR-021

Description: Doubling appears at the center of the middle marsh strip.

Die Indicators: Obverse Die chips appear above and northwest of the designer's initials JF.

Reverse A die chip appears near the heron's beak.

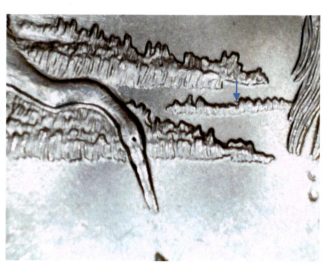
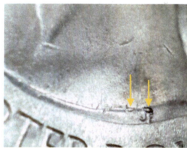
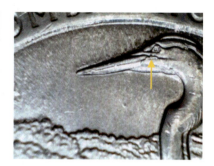

KENC 25¢ 2015 P DE DDR-022

Description: Doubling at an angle appears at the top of the middle marsh strip. This is similar to *KENC 25¢ 2015 P DE DDR-015*, but the doubling here is shorter in length.

Die Indicators: Obverse none observed

Reverse none observed

Description: Scattered doubling in the shape of an arch appears between the upper and middle marsh strips.

Die Indicators: Obverse none observed

Reverse Die chips appear on the heron's beak and face.

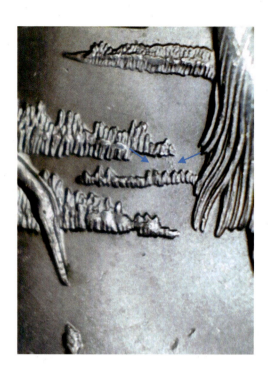

Description: Doubling appears below the upper marsh strip. Doubling shows at the center of the middle marsh strip.

Die Indicators: Obverse none observed

Reverse none observed

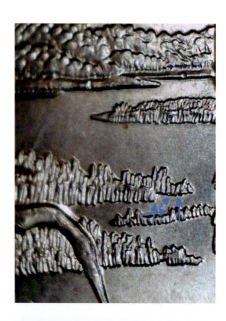

2015 New York Saratoga

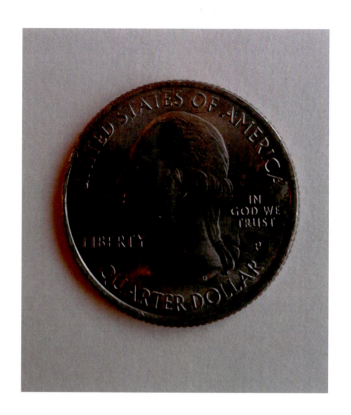 

Area(s) of Interest:

The lower right opening of the sword's guard

KENC 25¢ 2015 P NY DDR-001

Description: Doubling shows inside the upper right of the lower right opening of the sword's guard.

Die Indicators: Obverse none observed

Reverse A die chip appears on the sword's handle.

KENC 25¢ 2015 P NY DDR-002

Description: Doubling travels around the inside of the lower right opening of the sword's guard.

Die Indicators: Obverse none observed

Reverse none observed

KENC 25¢ 2015 P NY DDR-003

Description: Strong doubling shows inside the upper right of the lower right opening of the sword's guard.

Die Indicators: Obverse none observed

Reverse none observed

KENC 25¢ 2015 P NY DDR-004

Description: Doubling shows at the bottom of the lower right opening of the sword's guard.

Die Indicators: Obverse none observed

Reverse Die chips appear on the sword's handle.

Description: Doubling shows inside the upper right of the lower right opening of the sword's guard.

Die Indicators: Obverse none observed

Reverse A die chip appears on the sword's handle

Description: Doubling shows inside the upper right of the lower right opening of the sword's guard.

Die Indicators: Obverse none observed

Reverse none observed

2016 Illinois Shawnee

Area(s) of Interest:

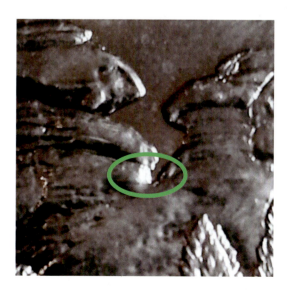

The bottom of the gap in the large rock formation

Description: Doubling shows as an extra rock at the bottom of the gap in the large rock formation.

Die Indicators: Obverse none observed

Reverse none observed

2016 Kentucky Cumberland Gap

 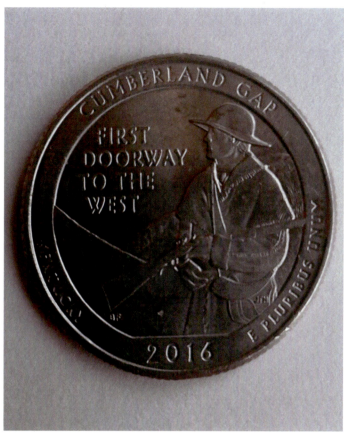

Area(s) of Interest:

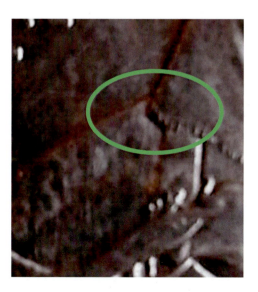

Below the fringe of the frontiersman's coat, Near the
intersection of the frontiersman's coat and mountain in the
background, Along the frontiersman's arm

KENC 25¢ 2016 P KY DDR-001

Description: Very close doubling shows on the fringe of the frontiersman's coat.

Die Indicators: Obverse none observed

Reverse none observed

KENC 25¢ 2016 P KY DDR-002

Description: Doubling shows as extra pieces of fringe from the frontiersman's coat appearing above the mountain.

Die Indicators: Obverse none observed

Reverse none observed

Description: Doubling shows along the frontiersman's coat, where the mountain and coat meet.

Die Indicators: Obverse none observed

Reverse none observed

Description: Minor doubling shows on the fringe of the frontiersman's coat directly above his arm.

Die Indicators: Obverse none observed

Reverse none observed

Description: Doubling shows along the fringe of the frontiersman's coat.

Die Indicators: Obverse none observed

Reverse none observed

Description: Close doubling shows along the frontiersman's coat, where the mountain and coat meet.

Die Indicators: Obverse Die chips and a die crack appear above the designer's initials JF.

Reverse none observed

KENC 25¢ 2016 P KY DDR-007

Description: Doubling shows along the fringe of the frontiersman's coat.

Die Indicators: Obverse A die chip shows northeast of the designer's initials JF.

Reverse none observed

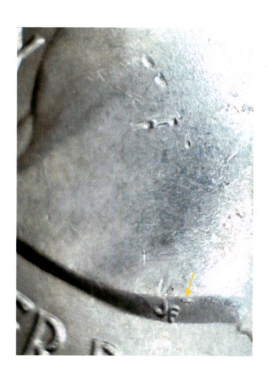

KENC 25¢ 2016 P KY DDR-008

Description: Doubling shows below the fringe of the frontiersman's coat and runs alongside his arm.

Die Indicators: Obverse none observed

Reverse none observed

Description: Doubling shows below the fringe of the frontiersman's coat and runs alongside his arm.

Die Indicators: Obverse none observed

Reverse none observed

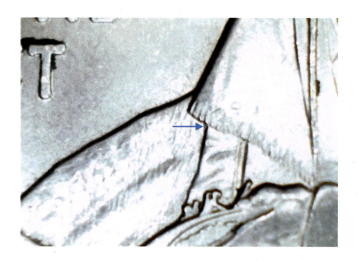

Description: Doubling shows below the fringe of the frontiersman's coat and runs alongside his arm.

2016 West Virginia Harpers Ferry

Window Numbers

Area(s) of Interest:

The window's above the left
doorway of John Brown's Fort

KENC 25¢ 2016 P WV DDR-001

Description: Doubling shows at the bottoms of windows 16 and 17. Doubling also shows along the left side of window 18 and along the left side of window 26.

Die Indicators: Obverse none observed

Reverse none observed

KENC 25¢ 2016 P WV DDR-002

Description: Doubling shows along the lower left side of window 14. Doubling also shows along the top and left side of window 22.

Die Indicators: Obverse none observed

Reverse none observed

KENC 25¢ 2016 P WV DDR-003

Description: Doubling shows along the bottom and right sides of windows 13 and 14. Doubling also shows in the top right corner of window 21.

Die Indicators: Obverse none observed

              Reverse A die chip appears along the right section of the fort's parapet.

KENC 25¢ 2016 P WV DDR-004

Description: Doubling shows along the tops and bottoms of windows 22 and 23. Doubling also shows along the lower right side of window 15.

Die Indicators: Obverse none observed

              Reverse none observed

KENC 25¢ 2016 P WV DDR-005

Description: Doubling shows along the tops of windows 14, 15, 22, and 23.

Die Indicators: Obverse none observed

Reverse none observed

KENC 25¢ 2016 P WV DDR-006

Description: Doubling shows along the top of window 22.

Die Indicators: Obverse Die chips and a die crack appear at the base of Washington's neck, left of the designer's initials JF.

Reverse none observed

KENC 25¢ 2016 P WV DDR-007

Description: Close doubling shows along the top of window 22.

Die Indicators: Obverse none observed

Reverse none observed

KENC 25¢ 2016 P WV DDR-008

Description: Strong doubling at an angle runs across window 23.

Die Indicators: Obverse A die crack runs along the base of Washington's neck left of the designer's initials JF.

Reverse none observed

KENC 25¢ 2016 P WV DDR-009

Description: Very close doubling runs along the right side of window 22, along the right side and bottom of window 14, and extremely close along the right side of window 6. Doubling in the left half of window 23 goes up and through window 15.

Die Indicators: Obverse A die chip touches the J of the designer's initials JF at the base of Washington's neck.

Reverse A die break appears on the right side of the fort northwest of the designer's initials PH.

KENC 25¢ 2016 P WV DDR-010

Description: Strong doubling shows in the lower portion of window 22.

Die Indicators: Obverse none observed

Reverse none observed

KENC 25¢ 2016 P WV DDR-011

Description: Doubling shows along the tops and right sides of windows 14 and 22. Doubling shows along the tops and left sides of windows 15 and 23.

Die Indicators: Obverse none observed

                      Reverse none observed

KENC 25¢ 2016 P WV DDR-012

Description: Doubling goes vertically through the center of window 22. Doubling goes vertically through the lower half of window 23.

Die Indicators: Obverse none observed

                      Reverse none observed

KENC 25¢ 2016 P WV DDR-013

Description: Doubling at a sharp angle appears in the top left corner of window 22.

Die Indicators: Obverse A die crack and die chips appear to the left and above the designer's initials JF on the base of Washington's neck.

Reverse none observed

KENC 25¢ 2016 P WV DDR-014

Description: Doubling runs along the bottoms of windows 22, 23, and 24.

Die Indicators: Obverse none observed

Reverse none observed

KENC 25¢ 2016 P WV DDR-015

Description: Doubling appears along the top and right side of window 22, along the right side of window 14, and along the tops of windows 15 and 23.

Die Indicators: Obverse none observed

                    Reverse none observed

KENC 25¢ 2016 P WV DDR-016

Description: Doubling travels around the bottom left corner of window 23.

Die Indicators: Obverse A die crack appears just above and left of the designer's initials JF on the base of Washington's neck.

                    Reverse none observed

 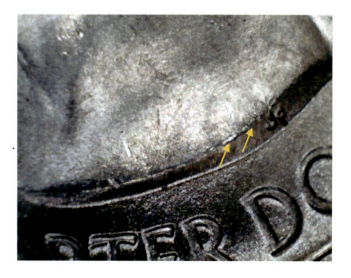

KENC 25¢ 2016 P WV DDR-017

Description: Doubling shows along the right sides of windows 21, 22, and 23.

Die Indicators: Obverse none observed

         Reverse none observed

KENC 25¢ 2016 P WV DDR-018

Description: Very close doubling shows along the top and left side of window 23.

Die Indicators: Obverse none observed

         Reverse A die break appears on the left section of the fort's parapet. A die chip appears on the right section of the fort's parapet.

Description: Doubling travels vertically through the center of window 22.

Die Indicators: Obverse none observed

Reverse none observed

Description: Doubling runs along the right side of window 21. Doubling runs along the top and right side of window 22.

Die Indicators: Obverse none observed

Reverse none observed

Description: Extremely close doubling appears along the tops of windows 22 and 23.

Die Indicators: Obverse A die crack starts left of and runs above the designer's initials JF.

Reverse none observed

KENC 25¢ 2016 P WV DDR-022

Description: Strong doubling appears in the lower portions and along the right sides of windows 14 and 15. Doubling also appears near the top right corner of window 22.

Die Indicators: Obverse Die chips and a die crack appear left of and on top of the designer's initials JF.

Reverse none observed

Description: Doubling runs along the top and right side of window 22, with the doubling running through into window 14. Close doubling appears at the bottom of window 15. Doubling runs across the top of window 23.

Die Indicators: Obverse none observed

                    Reverse none observed

Description: Close doubling at a slight angle appears on the lower left side of window 22.

Die Indicators: Obverse none observed

                    Reverse none observed

Description: Strong doubling runs horizontally across the upper portions of windows 22 and 23. Doubling also runs along the right sides of windows 22 and 23, with the doubling in window 22 going through the bottom right of the window.

Die Indicators: Obverse Die chips and a die crack appear left of and on top of the designer's initials JF.

                    Reverse none observed

Description: Doubling appears along the bottoms and right sides of windows 15, 22, and 23. Doubling appears along the bottom of window 14.

Die Indicators: Obverse none observed

                    Reverse none observed

KENC 25¢ 2016 P WV DDR-027

Description: Doubling appears along the right sides and bottoms of windows 13 and 21. Doubling covers nearly all of windows 14 and 22, with only the extreme left side of the windows showing the edge of where the doubling ends. Doubling shows along the bottom and right side of window 15. Extremely close doubling appears along the right side of window 23.

Die Indicators: Obverse none observed

Reverse none observed

KENC 25¢ 2016 P WV DDR-028

Description: Doubling goes vertically through the center of window 22. Doubling shows in the right half of window 23.

Die Indicators: Obverse Die chips appear left of the designer's initials JF at the base of Washington's neck.

Reverse none observed

Description: Doubling shows along the left side of window 15.

Die Indicators: Obverse none observed

Reverse none observed

2017 District of Columbia Frederick Douglass

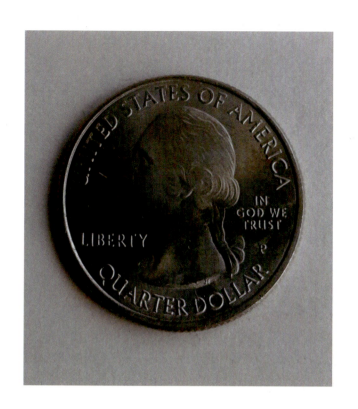 

Area(s) of Interest:

Near the bottom left window's shutter

Description: Doubling shows on the side of the house, to the right of the bottom left window's shutter

Die Indicators: Obverse none observed

Reverse none observed

2017 Missouri Ozark Riverways

Area(s) of Interest:

The cellar window

Description: Doubling appears as extra stones in the cellar window

Die Indicators: Obverse A die crack and die chips appear left of the designer's initials JF

Reverse none observed

KENC™ Coin Checklist

YEAR	MINT	STATE	VARIETY	IN COLLECTION ☑
1999	P	DE	KENC 25¢ 1999 P DE DDO-001	☐
1999	P	DE	KENC 25¢ 1999 P DE DDO-002	☐
1999	P	DE	KENC 25¢ 1999 P DE DDR-001	☐
1999	D	DE	KENC 25¢ 1999 D DE DDO-001	☐
1999	P	PA	KENC 25¢ 1999 P PA DDO-001	☐
1999	P	PA	KENC 25¢ 1999 P PA DDO-002	☐
1999	D	GA	KENC 25¢ 1999 D GA DDO-001	☐
2000	P	MD	KENC 25¢ 2000 P MD DDO-001	☐
2000	P	NH	KENC 25¢ 2000 P NH DDO-001	☐
2000	P	VA	KENC 25¢ 2000 P VA DDO-001	☐
2000	P	VA	KENC 25¢ 2000 P VA DDR-001	☐
2001	P	NC	KENC 25¢ 2001 P NC DDO-001	☐
2001	D	NC	KENC 25¢ 2001 D NC DDO-001	☐
2001	P	RI	KENC 25¢ 2001 P RI DDO-001	☐
2001	D	RI	KENC 25¢ 2001 D RI DDO-001	☐
2001	P	VT	KENC 25¢ 2001 P VT DDO-001	☐
2001	D	KY	KENC 25¢ 2001 D KY DDO-001	☐
2002	P	TN	KENC 25¢ 2002 P TN DDO-001	☐
2002	D	TN	KENC 25¢ 2002 D TN DDO-001	☐
2002	D	OH	KENC 25¢ 2002 D OH DDO-001	☐
2002	D	LA	KENC 25¢ 2002 D LA DDO-001	☐
2002	P	IN	KENC 25¢ 2002 P IN DDO-001	☐
2002	P	IN	KENC 25¢ 2002 P IN DDR-001	☐
2002	P	IN	KENC 25¢ 2002 P IN DDR-002	☐
2002	P	MS	KENC 25¢ 2002 P MS DDR-001	☐
2003	P	ME	KENC 25¢ 2003 P ME DDO-001	☐
2003	D	ME	KENC 25¢ 2003 D ME DDR-001	☐
2003	D	ME	KENC 25¢ 2003 D ME DDR-002	☐
2003	D	ME	KENC 25¢ 2003 D ME DDR-003	☐
2004	P	MI	KENC 25¢ 2004 P MI DDO-001	☐
2004	P	FL	KENC 25¢ 2004 P FL DDO-001	☐
2004	P	TX	KENC 25¢ 2004 P TX DDO-001	☐
2004	P	IA	KENC 25¢ 2004 P IA DDO-001	☐
2004	P	IA	KENC 25¢ 2004 P IA DDO-002	☐
2004	P	WI	KENC 25¢ 2004 P WI DDR-001	☐
2004	P	WI	KENC 25¢ 2004 P WI DDR-002	☐
2004	P	WI	KENC 25¢ 2004 P WI DDR-003	☐
2004	D	WI	KENC 25¢ 2004 D WI DDR-001	☐
2005	P	CA	KENC 25¢ 2005 P CA DDO-001	☐
2005	P	CA	KENC 25¢ 2005 P CA DDO-002	☐
2005	P	CA	KENC 25¢ 2005 P CA DDR-001	☐
2005	P	MN	KENC 25¢ 2005 P MN DDO-001/DDR-001	☐
2005	P	MN	KENC 25¢ 2005 P MN DDO-002	☐
2005	P	MN	KENC 25¢ 2005 P MN DDO-003	☐
2005	P	MN	KENC 25¢ 2005 P MN DDR-002	☐
2005	P	MN	KENC 25¢ 2005 P MN DDR-003	☐
2005	P	MN	KENC 25¢ 2005 P MN DDR-004	☐
2005	P	MN	KENC 25¢ 2005 P MN DDR-005	☐
2005	P	OR	KENC 25¢ 2005 P OR DDO-001	☐
2005	P	OR	KENC 25¢ 2005 P OR DDR-001	☐
2005	P	OR	KENC 25¢ 2005 P OR DDR-002	☐
2005	P	OR	KENC 25¢ 2005 P OR DDR-003	☐

YEAR	MINT	STATE	VARIETY	IN COLLECTION ☑
2005	P	WV	KENC 25¢ 2005 P WV DDO-001	☐
	P		KENC 25¢ 2005 P NE DDO-001	☐
2006	P	CO	KENC 25¢ 2006 P CO DDO-001	☐
2006	P	ND	KENC 25¢ 2006 P ND DDO-001	☐
2006	P	SD	KENC 25¢ 2006 P SD DDO-001	☐
2007	P	MT	KENC 25¢ 2007 P MT DDO-001	☐
2007	P	MT	KENC 25¢ 2007 P MT DDO-002	☐
2007	P	WA	KENC 25¢ 2007 P WA DDO-001	☐
2007	P	ID	KENC 25¢ 2007 P ID DDO-001	☐
2007	P	ID	KENC 25¢ 2007 P ID DDR-001	☐
2007	P	ID	KENC 25¢ 2007 P ID DDR-002	☐
2007	P	WY	KENC 25¢ 2007 P WY DDR-001	☐
2007	P	WY	KENC 25¢ 2007 P WY DDR-002	☐
2007	P	WY	KENC 25¢ 2007 P WY DDR-003	☐
2007	P	WY	KENC 25¢ 2007 P WY DDR-004	☐
2007	P	WY	KENC 25¢ 2007 P WY DDR-005	☐
2007	P	WY	KENC 25¢ 2007 P WY DDR-006	☐
2007	P	WY	KENC 25¢ 2007 P WY DDR-007	☐
2007	P	WY	KENC 25¢ 2007 P WY DDR-008	☐
2007	P	WY	KENC 25¢ 2007 P WY DDR-009	☐
2007	P	WY	KENC 25¢ 2007 P WY DDR-010	☐
2007	D	WY	KENC 25¢ 2007 D WY DDR-001	☐
2007	P	UT	KENC 25¢ 2007 P UT DDO-001	☐
2007	P	UT	KENC 25¢ 2007 P UT DDO-002/DDR-004	☐
2007	P	UT	KENC 25¢ 2007 P UT DDR-001	☐
2007	P	UT	KENC 25¢ 2007 P UT DDR-002	☐
2007	P	UT	KENC 25¢ 2007 P UT DDR-003	☐
2007	P	UT	KENC 25¢ 2007 P UT DDR-005	☐
2008	P	NM	KENC 25¢ 2008 P NM DDO-001	☐
2008	P	NM	KENC 25¢ 2008 P NM DDO-002	☐
2008	P	NM	KENC 25¢ 2008 P NM DDR-001	☐
2008	P	NM	KENC 25¢ 2008 P NM DDR-002	☐
2008	P	AZ	KENC 25¢ 2008 P AZ DDO-001	☐
2008	P	AK	KENC 25¢ 2008 P AK DDO-001	☐
2008	P	HI	KENC 25¢ 2008 P HI DDO-001	☐
2009	P	DC	KENC 25¢ 2009 P DC DDO-001	☐
2009	P	DC	KENC 25¢ 2009 P DC DDO-002	☐
2009	P	DC	KENC 25¢ 2009 P DC DDR-001	☐
2009	P	DC	KENC 25¢ 2009 P DC DDR-002	☐
2009	P	PR	KENC 25¢ 2009 P PR DDO-001	☐
2009	P	PR	KENC 25¢ 2009 P PR DDO-002	☐
2012	P	HI	KENC 25¢ 2012 P HI DDO-001	☐
2012	P	HI	KENC 25¢ 2012 P HI DDO-002	☐
2012	P	PR	KENC 25¢ 2012 P PR DDR-001	☐
2012	P	AK	KENC 25¢ 2012 P AK DDR-001	☐
2012	P	AK	KENC 25¢ 2012 P AK DDR-002	☐
2012	P	AK	KENC 25¢ 2012 P AK DDR-003	☐
2013	P	NH	KENC 25¢ 2013 P NH DDR-001	☐

YEAR	MINT	STATE	VARIETY	IN COLLECTION ☑
2013	P	OH	KENC 25¢ 2013 P OH DDO-001	☐
2013	P	OH	KENC 25¢ 2013 P OH DDO-002	☐
2013	P	OH	KENC 25¢ 2013 P OH DDO-003	☐
2013	P	OH	KENC 25¢ 2013 P OH DDO-004	☐
2013	P	OH	KENC 25¢ 2013 P OH DDR-001	☐
2013	P	OH	KENC 25¢ 2013 P OH DDR-002	☐
2013	P	OH	KENC 25¢ 2013 P OH DDR-003	☐
2013	P	NV	KENC 25¢ 2013 P NV DDR-001	☐
2013	P	NV	KENC 25¢ 2013 P NV DDR-002	☐
2013	P	NV	KENC 25¢ 2013 P NV DDR-003	☐
2013	P	NV	KENC 25¢ 2013 P NV DDR-004	☐
2013	P	NV	KENC 25¢ 2013 P NV DDR-005	☐
2013	P	NV	KENC 25¢ 2013 P NV DDR-006	☐
2013	P	MD	KENC 25¢ 2013 P MD DDR-001	☐
2013	P	MD	KENC 25¢ 2013 P MD DDR-002	☐
2013	P	MD	KENC 25¢ 2013 P MD DDR-003	☐
2013	P	MD	KENC 25¢ 2013 P MD DDR-004	☐
2013	P	MD	KENC 25¢ 2013 P MD DDR-005	☐
2013	P	MD	KENC 25¢ 2013 P MD DDR-006	☐
2013	P	MD	KENC 25¢ 2013 P MD DDR-007	☐
2013	P	MD	KENC 25¢ 2013 P MD DDR-008	☐
2013	P	MD	KENC 25¢ 2013 P MD DDR-009	☐
2013	P	MD	KENC 25¢ 2013 P MD DDR-010	☐
2013	P	SD	KENC 25¢ 2013 P SD DDR-001	☐
2013	P	SD	KENC 25¢ 2013 P SD DDR-002	☐
2013	P	SD	KENC 25¢ 2013 P SD DDR-003	☐
2013	P	SD	KENC 25¢ 2013 P SD DDR-004	☐
2013	P	SD	KENC 25¢ 2013 P SD DDR-005	☐
2013	P	SD	KENC 25¢ 2013 P SD DDR-006	☐
2013	P	SD	KENC 25¢ 2013 P SD DDR-007	☐
2013	P	SD	KENC 25¢ 2013 P SD DDR-008	☐
2013	P	SD	KENC 25¢ 2013 P SD DDR-009	☐
2013	P	SD	KENC 25¢ 2013 P SD DDR-010	☐
2013	P	SD	KENC 25¢ 2013 P SD DDR-011	☐
2013	P	SD	KENC 25¢ 2013 P SD DDR-012	☐
2013	P	SD	KENC 25¢ 2013 P SD DDR-013	☐
2013	P	SD	KENC 25¢ 2013 P SD DDR-014	☐
2013	P	SD	KENC 25¢ 2013 P SD DDR-015	☐
2013	P	SD	KENC 25¢ 2013 P SD DDR-016	☐
2013	P	SD	KENC 25¢ 2013 P SD DDR-017	☐
2013	P	SD	KENC 25¢ 2013 P SD DDR-018	☐
2013	P	SD	KENC 25¢ 2013 P SD DDR-019	☐
2013	P	SD	KENC 25¢ 2013 P SD DDR-020	☐
2014	P	VA	KENC 25¢ 2014 P VA DDR-001	☐
2014	P	UT	KENC 25¢ 2014 P UT DDO-001	☐
2014	P	UT	KENC 25¢ 2014 P UT DDR-001	☐
2014	P	UT	KENC 25¢ 2014 P UT DDR-002	☐
2014	P	UT	KENC 25¢ 2014 P UT DDR-003	☐
2014	P	UT	KENC 25¢ 2014 P UT DDR-004	☐
2014	P	UT	KENC 25¢ 2014 P UT DDR-005	☐

YEAR	MINT	STATE	VARIETY	IN COLLECTION ☑
2015	P	NE	KENC 25¢ 2015 P NE DDO-001	☐
2015	P	NE	KENC 25¢ 2015 P NE DDR-001	☐
2015	P	NE	KENC 25¢ 2015 P NE DDR-002	☐
2015	P	NE	KENC 25¢ 2015 P NE DDR-003	☐
2015	P	NE	KENC 25¢ 2015 P NE DDR-004	☐
2015	P	NE	KENC 25¢ 2015 P NE DDR-005	☐
2015	P	NE	KENC 25¢ 2015 P NE DDR-006	☐
2015	P	NE	KENC 25¢ 2015 P NE DDR-007	☐
2015	P	NE	KENC 25¢ 2015 P NE DDR-008	☐
2015	P	NE	KENC 25¢ 2015 P NE DDR-009	☐
2015	P	NE	KENC 25¢ 2015 P NE DDR-010	☐
2015	P	NE	KENC 25¢ 2015 P NE DDR-011	☐
2015	P	NE	KENC 25¢ 2015 P NE DDR-012	☐
2015	P	NE	KENC 25¢ 2015 P NE DDR-013	☐
2015	P	NE	KENC 25¢ 2015 P NE DDR-014	☐
2015	P	NE	KENC 25¢ 2015 P NE DDR-015	☐
2015	P	NE	KENC 25¢ 2015 P NE DDR-016	☐
2015	P	NE	KENC 25¢ 2015 P NE DDR-017	☐
2015	P	NE	KENC 25¢ 2015 P NE DDR-018	☐
2015	P	NE	KENC 25¢ 2015 P NE DDR-019	☐
2015	P	NE	KENC 25¢ 2015 P NE DDR-020	☐
2015	P	NE	KENC 25¢ 2015 P NE DDR-021	☐
2015	P	NE	KENC 25¢ 2015 P NE DDR-022	☐
2015	P	NE	KENC 25¢ 2015 P NE DDR-023	☐
2015	P	NE	KENC 25¢ 2015 P NE DDR-024	☐
2015	P	NE	KENC 25¢ 2015 P NE DDR-025	☐
2015	P	NE	KENC 25¢ 2015 P NE DDR-026	☐
2015	P	NE	KENC 25¢ 2015 P NE DDR-027	☐
2015	P	NE	KENC 25¢ 2015 P NE DDR-028	☐
2015	P	NE	KENC 25¢ 2015 P NE DDR-029	☐
2015	P	NE	KENC 25¢ 2015 P NE DDR-030	☐
2015	P	NC	KENC 25¢ 2015 P NC DDO-001	☐
2015	P	NC	KENC 25¢ 2015 P NC DDO-002	☐
2015	P	NC	KENC 25¢ 2015 P NC DDR-001	☐
2015	P	NC	KENC 25¢ 2015 P NC DDR-002	☐
2015	P	NC	KENC 25¢ 2015 P NC DDR-003	☐
2015	P	NC	KENC 25¢ 2015 P NC DDR-004	☐
2015	P	NC	KENC 25¢ 2015 P NC DDR-005	☐
2015	P	NC	KENC 25¢ 2015 P NC DDR-006	☐
2015	P	DE	KENC 25¢ 2015 P DE DDR-001	☐
2015	P	DE	KENC 25¢ 2015 P DE DDR-002	☐
2015	P	DE	KENC 25¢ 2015 P DE DDR-003	☐
2015	P	DE	KENC 25¢ 2015 P DE DDR-004	☐
2015	P	DE	KENC 25¢ 2015 P DE DDR-005	☐
2015	P	DE	KENC 25¢ 2015 P DE DDR-006	☐
2015	P	DE	KENC 25¢ 2015 P DE DDR-007	☐
2015	P	DE	KENC 25¢ 2015 P DE DDR-008	☐
2015	P	DE	KENC 25¢ 2015 P DE DDR-009	☐
2015	P	DE	KENC 25¢ 2015 P DE DDR-010	☐
2015	P	DE	KENC 25¢ 2015 P DE DDR-011	☐
2015	P	DE	KENC 25¢ 2015 P DE DDR-012	☐
2015	P	DE	KENC 25¢ 2015 P DE DDR-013	☐
2015	P	DE	KENC 25¢ 2015 P DE DDR-014	☐
2015	P	DE	KENC 25¢ 2015 P DE DDR-015	☐
2015	P	DE	KENC 25¢ 2015 P DE DDR-016	☐

YEAR	MINT	STATE	VARIETY	IN COLLECTION ☑
2015	P	DE	KENC 25¢ 2015 P DE DDR-017	☐
2015	P	DE	KENC 25¢ 2015 P DE DDR-018	☐
2015	P	DE	KENC 25¢ 2015 P DE DDR-019	☐
2015	P	DE	KENC 25¢ 2015 P DE DDR-020	☐
2015	P	DE	KENC 25¢ 2015 P DE DDR-021	☐
2015	P	DE	KENC 25¢ 2015 P DE DDR-022	☐
2015	P	DE	KENC 25¢ 2015 P DE DDR-023	☐
2015	P	DE	KENC 25¢ 2015 P DE DDR-024	☐
2015	P	NY	KENC 25¢ 2015 P NY DDR-001	☐
2015	P	NY	KENC 25¢ 2015 P NY DDR-002	☐
2015	P	NY	KENC 25¢ 2015 P NY DDR-003	☐
2015	P	NY	KENC 25¢ 2015 P NY DDR-004	☐
2015	P	NY	KENC 25¢ 2015 P NY DDR-005	☐
2015	P	NY	KENC 25¢ 2015 P NY DDR-006	☐
2016	P	IL	KENC 25¢ 2016 P IL DDR-001	☐
2016	P	KY	KENC 25¢ 2016 P KY DDR-001	☐
2016	P	KY	KENC 25¢ 2016 P KY DDR-002	☐
2016	P	KY	KENC 25¢ 2016 P KY DDR-003	☐
2016	P	KY	KENC 25¢ 2016 P KY DDR-004	☐
2016	P	KY	KENC 25¢ 2016 P KY DDR-005	☐
2016	P	KY	KENC 25¢ 2016 P KY DDR-006	☐
2016	P	KY	KENC 25¢ 2016 P KY DDR-007	☐
2016	P	KY	KENC 25¢ 2016 P KY DDR-008	☐
2016	P	KY	KENC 25¢ 2016 P KY DDR-009	☐
2016	P	WV	KENC 25¢ 2016 P WV DDR-001	☐
2016	P	WV	KENC 25¢ 2016 P WV DDR-002	☐
2016	P	WV	KENC 25¢ 2016 P WV DDR-003	☐
2016	P	WV	KENC 25¢ 2016 P WV DDR-004	☐
2016	P	WV	KENC 25¢ 2016 P WV DDR-005	☐
2016	P	WV	KENC 25¢ 2016 P WV DDR-006	☐
2016	P	WV	KENC 25¢ 2016 P WV DDR-007	☐
2016	P	WV	KENC 25¢ 2016 P WV DDR-008	☐
2016	P	WV	KENC 25¢ 2016 P WV DDR-009	☐
2016	P	WV	KENC 25¢ 2016 P WV DDR-010	☐
2016	P	WV	KENC 25¢ 2016 P WV DDR-011	☐
2016	P	WV	KENC 25¢ 2016 P WV DDR-012	☐
2016	P	WV	KENC 25¢ 2016 P WV DDR-013	☐
2016	P	WV	KENC 25¢ 2016 P WV DDR-014	☐
2016	P	WV	KENC 25¢ 2016 P WV DDR-015	☐
2016	P	WV	KENC 25¢ 2016 P WV DDR-016	☐
2016	P	WV	KENC 25¢ 2016 P WV DDR-017	☐
2016	P	WV	KENC 25¢ 2016 P WV DDR-018	☐
2016	P	WV	KENC 25¢ 2016 P WV DDR-019	☐
2016	P	WV	KENC 25¢ 2016 P WV DDR-020	☐
2016	P	WV	KENC 25¢ 2016 P WV DDR-021	☐
2016	P	WV	KENC 25¢ 2016 P WV DDR-022	☐
2016	P	WV	KENC 25¢ 2016 P WV DDR-023	☐
2016	P	WV	KENC 25¢ 2016 P WV DDR-024	☐
2016	P	WV	KENC 25¢ 2016 P WV DDR-025	☐
2016	P	WV	KENC 25¢ 2016 P WV DDR-026	☐
2016	P	WV	KENC 25¢ 2016 P WV DDR-027	☐
2016	P	WV	KENC 25¢ 2016 P WV DDR-028	☐
2016	P	WV	KENC 25¢ 2016 P WV DDR-029	☐
2017	P	DC	KENC 25¢ 2017 P DC DDR-001	☐
2017	P	MO	KENC 25¢ 2017 P MO DDR-001	☐